Never Lose a War

NEVER LOSE A WAR

Memoirs and Observations of a National Columnist

Holmes Alexander

FOREWORD BY
Barry Goldwater

DEVIN-ADAIR, PUBLISHERS
Greenwich, Connecticut

Manufactured in the United States of America.

Library of Congress Cataloging in Publication Data

Alexander, Holmes Moss, 1906–
  Never lose a war.

  1. Alexander, Holmes Moss, 1906–   .
2. Journalists—United States—Biography.   I. Title.
PN4874.A35A36   1984   070'.92'4 [B]   83-18964
ISBN 0-8159-6223-1

DEDICATION

CBA, Sr. (1876–1958)
CBA, Jr. (1905–1945, KIA)

DEVIN-ADAIR, PUBLISHERS, is America's foremost publisher of quality conservative books. Founded in 1911, the company has championed the cause of the Thinking Right and historically has published the work of major conservative writers. In recent years Devin-Adair has increased its emphasis in this area and today is considered the leading publishing firm of the right.

The firm also has a long standing reputation for works of significance in the fields of ecology, Irish literature, health, and nutrition. It publishes superbly illustrated nature and travel books on the Eastern seaboard through its Chatham Press subsidiary.

Devin-Adair's newest emphasis is in the area of books, programs, and software relating to the personal computer.

Devin-Adair operates the Veritas Book Club for conservative readers, the Ecological Book Club for nature and health audiences, and the Irish-American Book Society.

Publisher: C. de la Belle Issue
Managing Director: Roger H. Lourie
Cover Design: Michael Spizzirri
Book Design & Production: Arthur Hamparian
Typesetting: American Graphics Corporation

Devin-Adair, Publishers
6 North Water Street
Greenwich, Connecticut 06830

EXCELLENCE, SINCE 1911

Contents

Foreword by Senator Barry Goldwater   xi
Preface   xv

1. Ronald Reagan to the Saddle   3
2. Air Corps Experience   9
3. A Soviet Intervention   14
4. The Dog Tags   20
5. The Graveside   26
6. My Three Mentors   33
7. Normalcy and Peace   40
8. A Study in the Will to Win   47
9. Never Lose a War   54
10. The Truman Hammer   61
11. The Wildfire Spread of Internationalism   71
12. Fall of a Titan   85
13. War of Darkness at Home: I   98
14. War of Darkness at Home: II   110
15. The Losing Streak Begins   121
16. Faster Down the Chute   128
17. The Steepening Decline   138
18. How It Ends   147

Addendum: A Veteran Columnist Lays Down
    His Pen   153
Selected Bibliography   157

Foreword

THERE IS ALWAYS a certain sense of sadness as well as joy when reading the memoirs of one's contemporaries. The sadness comes from realizing that memoirs are written as the individual is bowing off center stage. The joy comes from knowing that the story being told is one that deserves to be told. I must confess that both of these emotions had their affect as I read *Never Lose A War*.

What is so ironic is that Holmes Alexander and I arrived in Washington about the same time and we will be leaving about the same time, albeit Holmes had a few more years at the start and finish than me. While his perspective was that of a newsman and mine was as a politician, nevertheless, our background and experience created a similar viewpoint on the United States and its role in world affairs.

In his memoirs, Holmes details the changes that have occurred in this country from the days of the Depression to the point where we are now. While it is written in the short, anecdotal style of a news column, nonetheless, the lessons and the meaning of what he has to say are abundantly clear. In documenting this period of time, he has delineated the forces and events that have changed our Nation forever, some good and some bad.

I think it is true that a person's moral characteristics are fashioned at a very early age. However, it is just as true that one's mental growth and processes never stop even while retaining those early, basic virtues. It is in this regard that I see Holmes' view on the domestic and foreign policies of this country.

On the domestic front, both of us remember World War I,

prohibition and the Depression. Both of us held high hopes that America was strong enough and self-sufficient enough to weather any storm. Yet, we both became disillusioned over the path that our government has taken. With a near total fixation on providing for the "care and feeding" of an individual from cradle to grave, our government has moved gradually, and in some cases by leaps and bounds, down the path to socialism and away from the concept of our Founding Fathers. By misapplying the "common welfare" clause of the Constitution, several Congresses, Presidents and the Courts have conspired to expand governmental functions at the expense of individual freedom. As Holmes has pointed out, the liberals of this country, while they profess great worry about the "little man," have absolutely no use for him other than to manipulate him for their own socioeconomic theories. Indeed, the self-styled liberals are the most illiberal people in this country, since they will not accept any criticism of their theories, especially from those they profess to help.

On the foreign policy front, it is obvious that Holmes, as well as most other Americans who lived through the time, has gone through a change caused by World War II. Up until 1941, the vast majority of Americans were content to keep their concerns and worries within the boundaries of the United States. On December 7, 1941, those dreams were shattered beyond repair and the United States was thrust upon the stage as a world superpower. Unfortunately, over the last 40 years, we have projected an up-and-down attitude toward this role in world affairs. Too often, we tend to criticize our government on a "damned if you do, damned if you don't" basis. It is in this area that *Never Lose A War* has a great appeal. With Holmes' newspaper style depicting the players on the scene, our policies and the decisions by which they are made take on a more human and personal touch.

The last thing I would like to touch on is Holmes' wartime experiences. I could not pass up the similarity between us with our Army Air Corps backgrounds. While Holmes was flying around in B-24s for the 8th Air Force, it could have been in a plane that I had ferried to Europe. And, like Holmes, my perspective on the world and the challenges facing America were greatly influenced by those days. Also, I have a sneaking suspicion that if all things had been equal, Holmes and I may have kept the wings on our breast pockets and would have "bored a lot of holes in the sky."

In any event, I am glad that Holmes chose to come to Washington and show us what the people are who make our laws and enforce them and interpret them. Also, I am glad that Holmes has decided to write this book for it belongs with any collection dealing with the comings and goings of our Capital City.

BARRY GOLDWATER

Preface

As a boy I frequently spent summers with relatives in Charles Town, West Virginia. At that time there were many Confederate veterans still around. Bitter over the South's defeat and the resulting tragedy of the ill-managed Reconstruction, one old warrior tendered me this oft-repeated warning: "Son, don't ever lose a war."

In calling this book *Never Lose A War*, I pass along that advice, because it seems to me that the U.S. may be about to lose a war— the one that began in 1945.

We had just subdued the Master Race and atomized the Sneak Attackers. We had military superiority, perhaps supremacy, on land, sea, and air. We held a monopoly on the ultimate weapon. But almost simultaneously that the West won World War II, we began losing the war we've been in ever since.

A piece here, a chip there, bit by bit, through default, stupidity, and disaffection, we've been handing over our American ideals to the neutralists, the peacemongers, and the One Worlders. My hope is that the good, decent, patriotic Americans who read this book will heed the warning, that what I have to say will strike some small spark to reinflame the American spirit.

If our children can say to their children, "No, we never *did* lose a war," then my purpose in writing the book will be more than gratified.

HOLMES ALEXANDER
Washington, D.C.

xv

Never Lose a War

1.

Ronald Reagan to the Saddle

WASHINGTON, D.C. 1/20/81. Last column after nearly 35 years. Ronald Reagan's Inaugural was my swan song, like poor pale Jimmy Carter's who sat on the dais with the President-elect.

Both principals, the attending multitude and the vast electronic audience were sweating out release of the 52 American hostages insultingly seized by pipsqueak Iran from the pitiful helpless giant. A great republic was in the throes of Decline and Fall. The incoming president promised to turn it all around, take the government off the backs of the people, stand up for America to all the world.

My grandmother had brought me to my first Inauguration, which was Wilson's second, March 4, 1917. Daughter and mother of congressmen, Mimi must have had clout, always sine qua non in Washington, for our seats were front and center. My mind was on matters more exciting than the presidential address. I'd read rumors that Wilson would be assassinated by German spies. I was bug-eyed over the Black Horse Troop of Culver Academy, and wanted to enroll there. My parents would decide on character-building Gilman Country School, Baltimore, Princeton University and Trinity College, Cambridge, England.

Reagan's first prescient break with the past was to hold the ceremonies on the Capitol's West Front, overlooking the marble city, the noble monuments, with National Cemetery in the distance. The first of my six inaugurals from the press-stands was Truman in '49. All you could see from the East Front of the Capitol were the Library of Congress, Supreme Court and Union Station. We'd been handed advance copies of his address

3

which we scanned. An adjacent reporter nudged me, "What do you see for a lead?" "Definitely, Point Four." It promised U.S. technical aid to all comers. You needn't have been clairvoyant, just "conservative," to foresee the results. Copying Franklin Roosevelt's federal welfare and international lend-lease, Truman would go on making dependents out of foreign nations and poor-mouthing Americans. Eisenhower, Kennedy, Johnson, Nixon, Ford and Carter ditto. Reagan was vowing to change all that.

Reagan's "Goldwater" telecast in 1964, much like Bryan's Cross of Gold extravaganza, created a determined White House porch climber. I was sure of Reagan's eventual success when I first heard him sound off. I flew to California to meet him and write him up. It was an instant and lasting congeniality. I left the inaugural hilltop with patriotic brine on my cheeks.

I'd fingered January '81, containing my 75th birthday and coinciding with Reagan's take-over, for the voluntary termination of my McNaught Syndicate contract. Others in my trade—Dorothy Thompson, Bill White, Joseph Alsop—had given advance notice to quit. It seemed a better ending than dropping dead like George Sokolsky or pooping out like David Lawrence. Hence, I'd written three predated columns to summarize the Washington experience. My friend, U.S. Senator Charles (Mac) Mathias of Maryland had entered the series in the *Congressional Record* as of 3/10/81. To sum up:

(1)

I value my life, and therefore abhor idleness and boredom. "When a man is tired of London, he's tired of life," declared Doctor Samuel Johnson. Same here. Lose your fascination with Washington, D.C. and you're done for. When the glamour goes, curtains . . . .

(2)

As the Hon. Barbara Jordan remarked on her retirement from the House of Representatives, the longer you stay in Congress, the harder it is to quit.

It's the same with quitting a syndicated column. All columnists, great and small, cling to the byline like a life raft. It takes an act of self-discipline to cast off and swim for it, even if you've been at it since 1946 and haven't set the lake afire or accumulated any delusions about being missed.

(3)

Note the difference—it has deep significance. When Harry Truman ran victoriously in 1948, he flogged the 80th Congress for being "no-account and do-nothing." When Ronald Reagan won in 1980, the 96th Congress was not so much vulnerable to demagogic blast as to God's wrath.

Seven members were under criminal indictment for bribery and conspiracy, one had been expelled by the House ethics committee and several others had been censored by their peers in various terms of disapproval. During that span (1948–80), it became reasonable to ask, "Is the United States capable of self-government?"

Washington journalism is a zoo with many species of the animal life. The nobility of the majestic lion and thoroughbred horse are there. The lesser breeds of harmless moo-cow and fawning lap-dog can be seen. The lower forms of jackal, viper and buzz fly are on exhibition along with the strutting peacock and the swollen toad.

No individual is free from the faults of the herd. The variety exists within the press corps because it resembles the meat it feeds on—the American political community, from the White House to the backstairs lobby.

Our ever-increasing access to the ballot box has progressively lowered the quality of our chosen leadership. We have beaten the bushes to bring out more voters: through women's suffrage, a lower eligibility age, the multilingual ballot, the outlawing of poll taxes, the liberation of residency requirements, the absentee ballot, the federal enforcement of voting rights and the federal subsidizing of candidates. All this has coincided with less participation on election day and plunging standards of decency and mentality in the winners.

Again, we see the animal fair of purebreds and mongrels, a menagerie where the democratic theory is debunked as quackery. The governing elite, the people's choice, is several cuts below the people themselves. Despite some splendid species that have paraded through the executive mansion, the congressional aisles, the persuasion parlors where legislators are massaged by Nobel prizemen as well as fleshpot merchants, national politics has become more and more a profession of, for and by the unclean. The bureaucracy, which is the servant class, draws undeserved salaries in protected jobs. These lackeys extend the absurd pretension of self-government as a human or philosophic value.

I would feel cowardly to end this valedictory without suggesting a remedy. Only yesterday I heard it seriously proposed that Richard Nixon be executed for his crimes against the American people, and that capital punishment be made the mandated penalty for all major offenses to the public good. Although not wholly won over to such extreme measures, I am not alone in the solemn conviction that a factor of authoritarianism must be introduced if the Republic is to survive. Not a dictator, but a take-charge ruler like the choleric Andrew Jackson or the adamant de Gaulle must be raised up.

Looking back on three decades of writing from the Washington beat, I cannot believe that it improved any talents I may have brought here, or that the political environment has been good for the men with whom I've worked. Rarely is there the likes of an Adam Smith, a Maynard Keynes, a Karl Marx, a Ben Franklin who develops from covering government. We feed on the material of legislation and administration which has little relation to eternal human verities.

Seldom does the byline correspondent meet with politicians whose sincerity is inviolate, whose purpose is undiluted patriotism, not mixed with trivial considerations and covert vanity. The wide world is not without hypocrisy in any society, but there is no worse offender than the society of politicians.

I left the welfare state of syndication, where publication is assured as long as the contract holds. I reentered the free-lance world of open competition. I wouldn't want to walk away without observing that I benefited from a special grace of our democracy—perhaps its saving grace. After all, a politician, Senator

Mac Mathias, put my diatribe into print in the *Congressional Record*, and the governmental publishers released and displayed it at taxpayers' expense. Such doings would be inconceivable under any system but ours. Mathias lived up to the letter and spirit of the First Amendment. He went the Second Mile. He introduced my columns in complimentary language and with his recommendations that his colleagues read and heed. The Maryland Senator is an exemplary solon, but not a solitary one. There is a working minority in both Houses who understands that America, this sick man of the Western World, will not be saved by stroking. The strong medicine of adversary criticism may, if there's still time, arouse the people to cleanse the temple. But Mark Twain long ago said that "there is no distinctly American criminal class except Congress." Does democracy work? Is the U.S.A. governable?

What's my excuse for this book? The clergy reminds us at funerals and other grave occasions that every man owes God a death. I am saying here that every journalist, obscure or illustrious, owes himself and interested bystanders a personal accounting.

I grew up in two West Virginia towns; Clarksburg, birthplace of Stonewall Jackson, Charles Town, locale for the trial and hanging of John Brown. My people had casualties, as well as leaders, in both Confederate and Federal service. I took strong "southerness" from my father. He, along with H. L. Mencken and historian Charles Beard, were the major influences of my thinking as it develops in these memoirs. When my family moved to Maryland during the Great War, my heart stayed behind. In a wartime Baltimore theater when the band played "Maryland, My Maryland," I sat with folded arms amid the standing crowd, such was my juvenile loyalty to the West Virginia Hills.

At 24, I was on the Democratic Boss's ticket and elected to the Maryland General Assembly. One campaign and one four-year term fixed my opinion of politics. I chose to be an observer of the sport, rather than a participant. I wrote two satiric articles, "I Run For Office" and "I Hold Office" in *Harpers* magazine, and got a five-book contract with Harper Brothers. I wrote short stories and articles for the slicks and the pulps. My interest split between horses, baseball and antics of politicians.

My first Harpers book was a biography of President Martin Van Buren, *The Red Fox of Kinderhook*. In 1939 Harpers arranged a fellowship for me to the Breadloaf Writers' Conference where I met celebrities—Bernard de Voto, J. P. Marquand, Robert Frost and lesser lights.

As my wife and I drove home in early September we heard the radio broadcast of England's declaration of war on Nazi Germany. I joined the Maryland State Guard and reactivated my ROTC lieutenancy. Like my father, Mencken, Beard and Charles Lindbergh, I was a Roosevelt-hater and isolationist, quite convinced that FDR had joined a war to beat a depression. I didn't know it, but my education in national and world affairs was beginning.

2.

Air Corps Experience

PASSES WERE CANCELED THAT AFTERNOON. "All personnel re-
stricted to the base." We knew what that meant. This was it. This
was our first mission. I had graduated from paddlefoot to part-
time air crewmember.

In the officers club that night we talked about it. Not much,
though, just a little. What was the use? Ever since arriving in
England we had been quizzing the men here ahead of us.
"What's it like?" we asked. The answers were singularly empty.
"What's it like? Well, pretty rugged sometimes." Or "Oh, I
dunno—not much future in it, I guess."

So now we were going to find out for ourselves. Letters were
written that night—very special letters which were handed to
non-flying friends with the nonchalant injunction "just in
case. . . ." For the rest, the mood was casual. Some went early to
bed; some played their usual rubbers of bridge; and those of us
who had to, went to work.

Shortly after midnight the crews were roused. The mission
would not go till dawn, but everyone would have plenty to do. We
at the intelligence office took sandwiches and coffee with maps,
charts and forecasts. The crews came slogging up the driveway
from the mess hall to the briefing room. An officer checked
them off at the door. "Empty your pockets . . . pick up an escape
kit . . . got your dog tags? Okay. Next."

The room filled quickly. It was cold in here. Men blew on their
fingers and rubbed their arms for circulation. They took their
seats by crews. I was flying today as aerial photographer.

9

We became silent as the operations officer stepped up on the low platform.

"Well, men," he said. "The 392nd is going to war today."

He gave a general outline of the mission and was followed by an intelligence officer, who dwelt upon the importance of the target and on what we might expect by way of opposition. We'd have Spitfire cover, he told us, against enemy fighters. There was a half-humorous murmur of satisfaction. And we could expect plenty of flak over the target. A dead silence. The weather officer came next; and finally the group commander. There was an expectant pause. After all, this was the first mission. Would we get a fight talk? The C.O. made his points—fly tight formation; don't go pot-shoting any friendly planes. "Everybody know what to do if he goes down in enemy territory?" Everybody did. "Any questions?" None. "Okay. Let's go."

In the drying room we dressed at wooden lockers from the skin out. Long-handled wool underwear, electrically heated flying suits, wool trousers and shirt, the winter flying suit of wool and leather, plus boots, a Mae West life jacket and a parachute. Outside on the trucks we had trouble getting our laden persons over the high tailboard. We boosted and pulled each other inside. The vehicles rumbled off toward the flight lines.

"Flak, huh?" mused someone from the dark interior of our truck. We all knew what he was thinking. Weren't we all?

The ground crew was busy at the plane, pre-flighting and bombing up. They had been at it most of the night. Our gunners hauled their pieces from the truck and went aboard. No gunner worth a damn will let another hand touch his weapon. The pilot stood by, clocking the work.

The work was finished. We held an impromptu meeting under the wing, running through signals before takeoff.

*   *   *

"Remember now," said the pilot. "Three buzzes on the emergency bell is the alert. One long buzz means—bail out."

"Except when there's a functional failure," put in the copilot. "In that case don't wait for the bell."

"Just what would you call a functional failure?" I anxiously asked.

"Well, for instance, if a wing falls off. . . ."

"Why don't we quit talking about these things," said the bombardier. "Let's talk about the *next* mission."

The meeting disbanded and we climbed aboard. In the waist with me were four gunners, two for the windows, one for the belly, one for the tail. We disentangled headsets and oxygen lines while up ahead the engines started. Our engineer who was using his pay allotments to buy a farm in California, came back for a final checkup.

We climbed up through the ground haze. There were other ships in the air, circling, but we couldn't see them for the mist. Suddenly we came out of it. Down below, through the patches of cloud was an incredibly beautiful picture. England in the morning. Wordsworth's sonnet: "Earth has not anything to show more fair. . . ."

Planes showed all about now as we joined the formation, still circling for altitude. I uncased my camera and took a few off-the-record shots. At 5,000 feet we passed above the temperate influence of the Gulf Stream and switched on our electric suits. When next I tried the camera, it was frozen stiff.

"Everybody under oxygen," came the order from the flight deck. The gunners took battle stations. "Best seat in the house," said the belly gunner as he crawled into his plexiglass bowl. Another went rear. Tail gunners, like southpaw pitchers, are a race apart. No sooner in his rotating turret than he opened up an inter-phone chatter.

". . . and lemme know when we cross the enemy coast," I heard him say.

"You'll *know* all right," somebody answered.

We were over water by this time. To the right, to the left, below us and above us, we could see the stepped-up formations of Allied bombers. It had been mentioned at the briefing that our outfit was part of a large striking force. But seeing was believing. To belong to this great sky-riding armada was to lose, temporarily at least, all sense of unit consciousness. There, visibly

and in multitude, was an air-borne battle fleet in which membership alone was honor enough.

Below was the enemy coast. I looked over the shoulder of the
left waist gunner just in time to see four evenly spaced flashes
three miles below us. Then I saw white puffs that expanded and
turned dirty in the sky—flak! For the first time in any of our lives
we were being shot at by an enemy. It was an exhilarating
sensation—the more so, I'm sure, because the enemy's aim was
very poor.

Then we saw fighters. Not theirs, but ours. We seemed to
know this instinctively, even before we caught the unmistakable
ellipse of Spitfire wings. Off to the right were dark ugly specks,
just as unmistakably enemy. Our formation closed a little tighter,
bracing for the attack. It never came. Not our guns, but the
eager Spitfires saw to that.

Bomb bay doors opened on the planes ahead. I crept out with
the K-2 hand camera on the quivering catwalk, but not before an
inner debate—should I wear my chute or not? "I'll tell you,
Alecks," the pilot had coached me, "if your chute snags on
something and comes open, you'll be pulled through the nearest
hold, regardless of how small." Also, a chute is cumbersome in
tight quarters and I needed to work the camera. So I skinned out
of the chute, lay on my belly amid the dangling 500-pound
explosives.

The oyster-shell doors opened beneath me. Green fields of
enemy made a picture of peace. Next in view was what the
briefing officer had called "a built up area"—some town of strategic value, I didn't doubt. Now we leveled off for the bombing
run. A metalic hiss signaled the electric release of our airborne
ammo. I wrestled with the frozen camera, but what fascinated
me was the slanting cascade of our bomb load—a geometric
pattern of swift and glittering beauty in the sky.

Cautiously I backed into the waist section with the gunners,
and got into the chute. I was remembering the briefing of heavy
flak over the target, and at that moment felt the ship stagger. It
rocked on its wings for a nervous moment, seemed to tremble,
then resumed an even pace.

The waist gunner nudged me and pointed downward. Leaning out, we watched dark objects falling from the rest of our formation, and puffs of antiaircraft artillery crackling in the sky. Our planes turned off target and I crossed to the position of the other waist gunner to see more loads strike home.

Some hours later we let down to our runways and saw them lined with comrades to welcome us back. Our first mission had been an easy one, as such things go—"a milk run." But just the same, these crews "had been there." "What's it like?" our friends ran up to ask. It was a familiar question that we'd asked of B-17 crews there before our B-24s. We heard ourselves giving familiar, elusive answers that we'd heard from others. Eager, talkative amateurs of the morning were veterans now—and inarticulate.

*   *   *

Ambiguous army regulations forbade us to keep diaries that might fall into enemy hands, yet we were encouraged to write morale-boosters for print back home—subject to censorship, the latter rife with the jealousy that overseas desk officers always held for the flyboys.

Determined not to cease being a writer, I bent the regulations by including action stories in letters to my father. He would have them censored by Zone of Interior officers who were responsible only to Washington, and send them out to editors.

As a result, I kept up these first-person yarns which appeared in the *Baltimore Evening Sun,* Mencken's page, and in the big circulation *Saturday Evening Post* which published them in miniature editions throughout the European Theater of Operations.

3.

A Soviet Intervention

PRESIDENT ROOSEVELT WAS DEAD. The European war was over.
Discipline, never very confining in the Eighth Air Force, became
permissive. Many of my officer friends went to London to watch
Churchill appear on the Buckingham Palace Balcony with the
royal family. Others went to Paris where the joy was less refined.
I didn't feel like celebrating in view of some news from home.

It was not hard news, but only a message of uneasiness. My
parents relayed vague reports about my brother Charles. He had
a trick baseball knee and was rejected as 4-F and signed on as a
front line ambulance driver. One day I landed from a mission
and heard from the ground crew of an invasion of southern
France—reportedly a soft one.

It suited me to hear that because I knew that Charles, having
been through African and Italian campaigns, was part of this
new thrust into Germany. He and I had corresponded while he
was somewhere in the Black Forest. He said he'd return home at
war's end through England and pay me a call.

Civilian by American status, Charles was a simulated lieutenant in the French medical corps. He commanded a squad or two
of Senegalese whose colonial master encouraged them to rape
and plunder. Somehow, since Charles didn't carry a gun into
battle, there had been less apprehension at home about his
service than mine, though I never saw a battlefield and he saw
little else. But the American Field Service was amateur-run.
Messages to Baltimore were vague about his whereabouts and
welfare, and sent as such by V-mail to me.

I was uneasy rather than anxious about him. Charles was a

14

merrymaker, a prankster, and I fully expected him to turn up at his Headquarters wearing an Arabian fez or some outrageous African costume. Or, since the Germans were deserting en masse to escape the Russian advance, I could easily imagine Charles marching a gaggle of prisoners into an Allied depot.

Instead of going to the V-E celebrations, I went with three friends to Stratford-on-Avon (my second visit of this tour of duty) and caught a Shakespeare comedy. It gave me a chance to stop at the London Field Service office. I asked for news of Charles. There was none. I was told to leave a telephone number where I could be reached. I gave the number of Headquarters, Maj. Gen. Laurence Kepner, commanding, knowing his adjutant would find me.

On a bright summer morning, 1945, I volunteered to take what promised to be a safe, sightseeing flight. It was to go from the Norwich area of England into what had been Hitler's Festung Europe. The clothing this time was not battle dress. It would be enough to pull zippered coveralls over the uniform and to don a leather flight jacket. I drew a back-parachute and reported to the briefing room.

I needed a boredom breaker. We of the 2nd Air Division were awaiting trans-shipment to the Pacific theater where presumably I would do Air Sea Rescue. I had a special interest because Far East water distances were greater. Helicopters had been introduced there, and I had never seen one. For the most part, these were idle days, with some desultory lecturing of bored crews. In my case, there were flying lessons with pilots who needed air time to draw their extra-hazardous pay.

Somebody high up—Marshall or Roosevelt—had permitted the Ruskies the honor of taking the Fascist capital. In our Britain-based Eighth Air Force we had mostly hearsay about the Soviet's contribution to the war effort. There had been some goodwill shuttle missions—B-17s over Berlin eastward to refueling stops in Russia, home by way of Italy. Our B-24s had not participated to my knowledge. I had been afoot in Liege and Brussels on some vague business of the German V-rocket sites. I had been no further eastward except in a raid near Hanover to bomb the factory of an enemy weapon which our side could not yet match—the jet fighter plane. Many of us were asking what would have happened if Hitler had developed the rocket and the jet a little earlier. We did not guess that we had our own supposedly-secret weapon, the atomic one, nor that we had another enemy, as yet unmasked, the Slavic one.

This morning at the briefing we had strangers on the benches ordinarily occupied by combat crewmen. The newcomers were non-flying troops from the Army Signal Corps. Their weapons were a variety of still and movie cameras. The briefing officer said something like this: "Men, this is a reconnaissance mission over Germany. We won't carry bombs. We won't mount machine guns. Only your cameras. SHAPE Intelligence wants information about bomb damage. What strategic effect did the B-24, B-17 raids have on German industry, transportation and troop concentrations? Our regular pilots, co-pilots and navigators will fly you over the targets that we've been hitting for more than two years. Top headquarters will study your photo intelligence to learn more about air power."

He paused and shuffled among the notes on his lectern. I knew all he had told us thus far, but not what was next and final.

"Men, we have some explicit instructions. I'm talking now to those who will be operating the planes. All targets are clearly marked on your maps. You may fly as low as 400 feet over the targets where there's clear weather, as we expect. If there's cloud cover or other obstructions, skip that target. Take no chances. We'll go back another day. Now, get this. Whatever you do, do not—repeat, do not—fly east of the Elbe River. Any questions?"

No questions. "Dis-*miss*."

We rode trucks to the runway. The Signal Corps men and their gear went aboard first. I swung up through the escape hatch into the belly of the lead plane. The waist section of the plane was congested with the extra personnel and equipment. I put on earphones and a throat mike to communicate with the deck. In a few minutes we were airborne. The green and pleasant land of England fell beneath.

We pushed out over the cold gray of the North Sea. Soon would be the landfall of the Frisian Islands. Beyond that was a land whose very name once chilled the airman's and the soldier's heart—Germany.

Flying at a comfortable altitude of 2,000 feet we would be the better part of two hours before reaching the target area. As always when uneventfully airborne, I allowed myself to muse and reminisce.

Home. It was a high frequency word in my thoughts. I remembered that four years prior to this plane ride into Germany, I had written a pre-Pearl Harbor piece intended for the *Baltimore Evening Sun,* "One for Isolation." I was rebutting a staff-written column, "One for Intervention." Mine was strictly an off-beat attitude in early 1941. I had cast my first vote in 1932 for Roosevelt; and ever since had regretted it. I joined the Liberty League, campaigned for its slate and for Willkie. Meanwhile I had met Charles Beard, a rampant isolationist, and I became the steadfast disciple of Henry L. Mencken, our prize iconoclast.

By 1940 I had seen Roosevelt break the third term ban, join the Atlantic war against Germany, commence a *de facto* alliance with Russia and bend his Far East diplomacy to defend what Mencken called "The moth-eaten pirate flag of Britain." In "One for Isolation" I ridiculed the weak infantilism of crawling back into the Mother Country's womb. Let America grow strong enough to stand alone, independent of entangling alliances.

As great a man as Charles Lindbergh believed as I did. Riding the rockabye reconn flight into Germany, I recalled how Lindbergh had been smeared as a Fascist and a Jew-baiter and lost his commission. His mistreatment persuaded me to withdraw "One for Isolation." I filed it in an upright steel cabinet with other unpublished manuscripts, marking it "Withheld for prudential reasons." I did not choose to risk my lieutenant's bars.

"Pilot calling. We're coming up on Target One."

I made encouraging motions to the Signal Corpsmen to man their cameras. The low-level flying over a tossing landscape proved too much for them. The plane's flooring became slippery and malodorous with vomit. I had a light stomach for that, and thrust my head out the hatch when there came another call from the flight deck.

"Major, sir?"

"Go ahead, pilot."

"Lieutenant Flannigan in the plane off our right wing has a message. He says that's Magnaburg below, only about 60 miles to Berlin which he's bombed from four miles up. He wants to fly in at low altitude and see what the hell Big B looks like."

I answered, "Back to pilot. You remind Flannigan [not his name] of what the briefing officer said. We were told, don't— repeat, don't—fly east of the Elbe River. Tell Flannigan to carry on as before."

There was a long pause. From the plane window I saw Flannigan's ship veer off and turn eastward. Over the intercom: "Major, sir. I gave him your message. He says a close look at Big B is something he can't pass up."

It was not a convenient place or time to pull rank.

"Roger, pilot. Proceed on course."

We were another two hours or so over the old targets west of the Elbe River. We banked for a return to base. It was late in the afternoon when we put down—three planes instead of four. Consternation was the mood as we gathered for the debriefing. Where was Flannigan? Why hadn't I stopped him? Didn't I know the Elbe River was the frontier between the Russian forces and the Western allies?

We hadn't been told that in the morning. It was news to me. After a certain amount of wrangling, I went to the officers club for the evening chow, but questions pursued me. I was an oldster among my mates, known to be a teacher and a writer. I was supposed to have the answers.

"How about those Ruskies? Aren't they our allies? What's the idea of shooting down a low-flying, unarmed plane?"

"I wish I knew."

"Alecks, look. We ought to drive the Russians back to Russia. We've got the airpower in Britain, in Germany and in Italy. We've got the armies of Ike and Monty. We've got control of the seas. We ought to get tough while we're strong."

How many times in the peace that lay ahead would those demands be voiced! "Drive the Russians back to Russia. . . . Get tough while we're so strong." Yes, but already in the press and over the radio, we could hear the chant, "Bring the boys home."

Someone had added a much-heard verse to the popular all-nation song of "Lili Marlene."

> "Oh, Mr. Truman, why can't we go home?
> We have licked the Master Race,
> Rubbed it out without a trace!
> When do we go h-o-m-e?
> Why can't we go h-o-me-ee?"

Amidst this quizzing and banter in walked Flannigan. We got his story. Flying low, slow and defenseless, he drew a volley of ground fire. Then he was bulldogged by several MIG fighters. Either because of damage, or warning, or discretion, Flannigan's crew made a forced landing. They had been trucked back across the river, and turned over to a British air station.

Everybody looked to me for explanation. I had none. Ahead of me, back home, lay a 30-year hitch at commentary writing. I would always wonder whether Soviet Russia was an ally or an enemy which would expand and defend its frontier as far as American inaction would permit.

4.

The Dog Tags

DEATH IS THE UNIVERSAL ABSOLUTE. Roosevelt was dead; so was my brother Charles, almost simultaneously, not long before V-E Day. Charles had served in Africa, Italy and Europe as a frontline ambulance driver in the American Field Service, which is why the news came to me as it did. Hastening toward me at my BOQ, General Kepner's adjutant lifted a salute, and even before returning it, I knew he brought bad news.

"Alecks," he said, "I've got to give you this exactly as it came to me. Your brother was captured shortly before the fighting ended. He died of wounds."

There is no way to give bad news. I actually felt sorry for this messenger of death. But then the content of his message hit me and I walked in a daze to my quarters. There I unpocketed the letters just received.

The first I opened was dictated by my father to his secretary. It was typically direct and succinct. The New York headquarters, American Field Service, had telephoned him to say that his son and a companion had been shelled while in a jeep at the front line in southern Germany. Both had been wounded, taken prisoner, but treated as non-combatants. My brother's companion returned to his own lines. Charles remained in enemy custody. He was not thought to be in critical condition. If I could learn more, my father asked, please communicate.

The next letter, from my wife, written two days later, was as typical of her as was the other missive of its writer. Mary's began, "Darling, your poor brother has been killed in battle." Sensibly, she did not write what she told me later. It was that my unhappy

20

mother had telephoned the War Department requesting my immediate return to comfort her distress. She was accustomed to special privilege. The European War was over, but she had premonitions that both her sons abroad would be killed.

My own state of mind was not helped by what I had heard of German bestiality and the fact that Charles had commanded African mercenaries who were paid in part by the freedom to rape and pillage. I could think of nothing but to get to a Red Cross station in our headquarters. I walked into that hutment and found it in the charge of a gray-uniformed girl.

"Oh, major, I'm so sorry. What can I do?"

I said the American Field Service kept a London office and that a Red Cross call might get some facts. She promised to make the call. I thanked her and went listlessly to the mess and ate in silence. Nobody here knew Charles and I had no wish for discussion until I spotted across the room a merry, round, frost-colored face, our Catholic chaplain. Chappie was everybody's buddy regardless of religion. In particular he was mine because of something that once happened.

Back during the second anniversary of our 392nd Bomb Gp. (H) of B-24 Liberators (aircraft nobody ever seems to write about) I was called by the C.Q. for the birthday mission. I went chattering in the predawn chill to the shower room. There I hung my plastic dog tags over the spigot. I don't recall ever doing this before; it certainly was not habitual, a strange, maybe ominous departure from the norm. In the briefing room we saw from the wall maps that the mission was deep, and learned from the briefing that we were to hit a jet plane plant (something new to us) and to expect fighter jet interception, also a novelty.

Only then, patting my chest for the familiar discs, did I miss them and recall where I'd hung them. I was startled by my behavior. Some tricks the subconscious will play. Was it only an honest oversight that had caused me to walk away from my tags? What made me clap my chest after learning of the ruggedness of the mission? Soldiers are warned, early and late, never to be parted from their identification discs. Caught without them behind enemy lines would make a man liable for execution as a spy.

Plainly I had an excuse for bugging out. There wasn't time to retrieve the tags. No superior, if notified, would let me go aboard. There were certain to be cynics (some with a guilty conscience) who would say that I had had a memory lapse on purpose.

As these thoughts raced through my head, I saw the Romish clergyman finishing the usual rites to his kneeling communicants and stepped beside him.

"Chappie, I'm in a jam."

Quickly I told him. Without a word he opened his collar, peeled loop and two discs over his head. He lowered his face above them in a blessing and said without a false note in his voice,

"Well, Alecks, take mine."

I ducked my own head while he slipped the objects over my neck. I tucked the discs into my clothing.

"Thanks, Chappie. You know I'm not of your faith."

"God bless you and keep you, with all the rest," he answered.

It was wonderful to feel that the chaplain, wise to all the pretensions of men, never thought to doubt me, but there was more to come. In the tight-packed trucks, standing in our heavy clothes, cuddling our parachutes, we rumbled to the armament shack. Here each gunner leaped out and picked up his .50 calibre gun-barrel; the rest of the weapon and the ammunition would already be aboard the ship. A master sergeant stood at the exit for a final check.

"All right, now. Got your dog tags? Got your escape kit? Oxygen mask? Roger. Next."

My turn came to pass him.

"Okay, sir. Hey, hold on. That oxygen mask is several issues out of date. Here, take a new one."

"This one's been good luck for me, sarge. I'd just as leave use it again."

"Hell, it's a damned antique. Treat yourself to the best."

He thrust a cardboard box into my arms and took the old mask. We remounted the truck, trundled off to the runway where we clambered aboard our designated planes. I attached the machine gun barrel to its mounting at the right window and fed ammunition into the conveyor belt from a metal container on the floor. Somebody said, "Hey, we may be scrubbed. The navigator says so. The poop from Group is that the weather's coming down. We may not go up."

"Lord," I thought, "let's don't scrub this one."

I wanted to go. It is like getting a girl up on her toes—you've got to kiss her. Those damned dog tags! I was better off with Chappie's than with none. But what if I had to jump? Would my captors believe me to be a priest? Maybe I'd be shot for an imposter anyhow. I didn't really believe this, but it gave me one of those graveyard chuckles.

A moment later the first of the four big engines coughed, sputtered and roared. The mission evidently would go.

Our B-24, crammed with blockbusters, sky markers, signal flares, extra ammo and a new flak-fooler called "chaff" waddled into place. It picked up motion, gathered speed, became airborne. On that morning, I felt more than ever proud just to be a crew member and an American. It struck me hard how much my country was giving to set the world aright.

We began the slow circling climb to find our altitude and our position in the vast formation. I steadied the swaying machine gun against my stomach and used both hands to adjust the new mask. I tugged the strap next to my right ear. A cold horror shot through my vital parts. Horrors! The strap broke! It came off in my hand!

I stared at the broken strap. Unless the mask was firmly in place across my nose and mouth, I surely would perish of anoxemia before finishing this eight-hour flight. There was an SOP (standing operating procedure) that applied. A useless crewmember should not continue on a combat mission as extra weight. The SOP required me to bail out while still over Britain and report back to the base.

There were precedents, but I could only think of one, and it wasn't enough. A few weeks ago Captain Jim Myers, a pilot, had lost two engines on takeoff. It would have been senseless to continue the long mission, but he could not land with a full load of bombs and .50 calibre ammo. Jim managed to circle aloft while the whole crew jumped to safety. He dumped his bombs in the open sea and brought the ship home on two feathered props.

Sound judgment and cool performance were expected of us, but my problem was full of plus and minus signs. If I bailed out, the place would be relieved of excess weight, but there would be an unmanned gun against the newfangled jets. The wily Luftwaffe had proved capable of spotting a deserted gun position and attacking there. If the plane went down I would be the crew's only survivor. Better stay by the gun as long as possible, even in enemy terrain.

Meanwhile, as a makeshift, I pressed my face against the skin of the plane to hold the mask in place. With infinite relief, I saw the red bouncing ball that indicated the inhalation of oxygen. Given luck, I wouldn't need the broken strap. As it happened, I got an irritating frostbite across my cheekbone and nose—my only "wound."

"Pilot to waist."

"Go ahead, pilot."

"You may clear your guns now."

"Roger, pilot."

I squeezed the electric trigger and felt the reassuring throb of the powerful weapon; I smelt the cordite from the rising heat of the fired gun. I watched the tracers bend through the sky. It was only a routine checkup, a round of warm-up, but I felt myself restored to the crew which I almost had left.

There was plenty of shooting in earnest that day. The Luftwaffe dived. The flak came up. Our fighter escort of P-51s, only half as fast as the opposition, darted in and out at the German fighters. We opened the floor hatch and tossed out the metalized strips that we called Christmas tree "chaff." It proved extraordinarily effective in misguiding the enemy's radar-directed fire. We took a hit in the bomb bay that exploded the skymarkers and signal flares. The waist section was incarnadined with thick crimson smoke. The pilot inter-comed from the flight deck, "Anybody alive in the waist?" We were scared but unscathed. The blood red smoke blew away.

We were back over the home base exactly on our ETA. The most welcome sight I recognized was the silvering oval of Chappie's face. He lifted his hand, and dangled a plastic cord with metal discs.

"Found 'em in the shower room," he laughed. "Thought you'd like them back."

All this took place several months before I got the death message on Charles. That night, I went to Chappie's quarters and told him what I had learned about it.

"Dammit," I said, "the war was practically over when this happened. If Charles had stayed out of the fighting a little longer, it wouldn't have happened."

"Maybe not," he said. "We never know."

I honestly forget whether he offered to pray for Charles's soul, but I'm sure that he did, and that I must have joined him.

5.

The Graveside

On the day after my talk with Chappie, a phone call reached me from the London office of the ambulance field service. The spokesman was sympathetic. He gave me some details as to time and geography. He said that Charles's friend and mine, Robertson (Bobby) Fenwick of the Green Spring country back home had been serving with my brother at the time of death. He knew all the circumstances, was passing through England en route to America, and would like to see me. I welcomed the opportunity, and arranged to meet Bobby at the Red Cross in downtown Norwich.

In the interim I attempted to make my letters home more heartening than my own feelings. I went back to thinking of my first novel I had written at Cambridge, *Twenty of Their Swords* (1930), with its theme of star-crossed lovers in predestined tragedy. My scholarship was not deep or broad enough to support the thesis. Over the years I had read dozens of academic philosphers and creative writers who plumbed the depths. Some found the universe to be callous, some sadistic. Others postulated that there are individuals who live under a hereditary curse, or are pursued by a Nemesis or incubus, while the rest of us enjoy some measure of free choice. Historians have similar beliefs about nations and their influence from environment. In *Tomorrow's Air Age* (1953) I was close enough to World War II to hold strong opinions. I wrote:

"Surely it is no accident that Germany has produced more than its share of mischief-makers. The gloomy philosophers of metaphysics and nihilism, Marx, Nietzsche and Kant—all Ger-

26

mans—cannot be wholly disconnected from the homeland conditions of storm and murkiness."

My central interest in June 1945 was Charles, the affectionate laugher and innocent joker who we never thought of as having a serious bent. But I recollected as I used my personal journal for solitary cogitation what Mary had said to me as we drove home from Charles's wedding. The ceremony was flawed by bigotry on both sides because his bride was Catholic. I felt for him that day. Mary had said, "Everybody seems to think of Charles as a happy-go-lucky chucklehead, but I never have."

"What do you mean?"

"I mean that he hides under that buffoonery. He has pessimism that doesn't show."

How could she tell, if she did? This affable, gregarious brother had seemed to breeze through school, college and business without a worry except for athletic injuries that dogged him. I had not seriously thought till his death of Mary's observation, and now I believed that she was speaking with knowledge out of her depths. She had attempted suicide in her nervous breakdown. I felt there was more insight behind those gray-green eyes than in all the books and sermons I'd known. She loved life, yet did not value her own when it became a burden. Years later I would write about her from the awe of love. And of my father and mother when they were dead. Of him, I had praise for the stoic fortitude, Hemingway's "grace under pressure." Of my mother, I felt that her trivial, harmless, feminine vanities had been overpunished by sorrow and lingering death, making God a less humane judge than human ones.

Bobby Fenwick and I met on schedule. I brought him back with me to Division Headquarters. This slim, empty-sleeved, pink-cheeked youth had lost an arm at birth. He enlisted in battlefield service that showed him more death and destruction than I had any reason to encounter. The gist of his story was that Charles had died of German shellfire, in German hands, been hurriedly buried, once in a corner of the battlefield, later in a village graveyard.

"German soil?" I asked.

"Yes."

"Well, Bobby, that won't do."

"I knew you'd feel that way. It's why I came to tell you. If there's transportation there and back, I can take you to the churchyard. I suppose we could move the body to an American cemetery."

* * *

Personal Journal

Hdqtrs., 2 A.D., June '45. Orders were issued by General Kepner. On 4 June Bobby and I left by plane (Dick Brandt, pilot, and Carl Berthell, navigator) for Charleroi, I having been assigned on T.D.Y. (temporary duty) to the Eighth Fighter Command in France.

June 5. Flew from Brussels to Paris to Graves Register. Wrote letter of explanation and received written authority to remove body.

June 6. Traveled by train to Strasbourg.

June 7. By field ambulance from Strasbourg to Baden Baden, headquarters of Charles's outfit. Met his section fellows, all handicapped persons who had volunteered for the grisly work of mercy.

How they loved, admired and missed him. Easy to see what a real friend and leader he had been.

June 8. With Bobby drove in ambulance through the mountains and over rough country to Neiderbonn, Alsace, to the American military cemetery there. Arranged for a grave and for a burial squad of one corporal and two Italian cooperators. Planned to leave in the morning.

Bobby had to return the borrowed ambulance. I stayed at the American air base of Hancheau where I got a truck and driver and arranged to have a chaplain at the grave.

June 9. Picked up grave detail and drove to Niefern. Bobby was waiting there at the village cemetery in a jeep. My burial detail included a sergeant with an automatic rifle to guard us and the vehicle. Surrounded by a crowd of curious and sullen Germans, I went into the churchyard and put a longhandled shovel into the soil of a fresh grave.

There was a shuffling and murmur from the German crowd.

Some cried out, "Nein. Nein." I stepped back and pointed to the grave, "Das ist mein brudder." Immediately, there was a rising murmur of protest followed by ejaculations of relief. An emaciated man with a limp arrived with a villager who had run to fetch him here. The new arrival said in English,

"Sir, there was an American put into the grave. It was your brother. I helped to bury him. But later some of your soldiers came and exhumed him. They took his body to an American cemetery—at a place near Ulm. It is a German boy in that grave."

I asked if there were any papers to verify the story. The spokesman said he would satisfy me if I came to his house. Leaving Bobby at the vehicle with the armed soldier and burial detail I followed the English-speaking villager to a small dwelling and to a cramped inner room. I won't say I was without misgivings. This was an enemy land, though now at peace, and I was in a uniform these people had reason to hate. But the person who limped with me was of an extraordinarily gentle mien, perhaps that of a pastor or physician, and I was a determined hunter by this time. He bade me sit on a broken divan, fumbled into a rolltop desk and brought out a bundle of tied papers. As soon as he opened this before me, I saw my brother's belongings—some family pictures, a batch of letters, one or two from me, and a leatherbound diary, secured by elastic bands.

The German homeowner said, "And there was a pocketbook, with dollars and francs, and an American passport. These I mailed to the Geneva International Red Cross. It was as he asked."

"He asked?" I repeated.

"He had been left in the jeep where he was shot. I think there was some firing and the German soldiers ran off. I believe they thought his friends would come and take him. But he was wounded in the chest. I carried him into this house. I called him his name—Charles. What a tall, strong man! He asked me, 'Must I die?' When I nodded, he told me his wife was to get the objects you hold, and the rest I sent to Geneva. I held him, as he died. We buried him in the field, and later at the church."

There was no doubting the man's sincerity and kindness, and

no mistaking the objects he had for proof. I could only be grateful that my brother had this comfort in his dying moment, incongruous as it seemed in the depth of Germany. I went back to Bobby. We dismissed the military detail. He drove me to a riddled, burned-out jeep in an open field. I picked up a spent fragment on the floor, and dropped it in my pocket.

Bobby said, "He was fired on by a mortar that was behind the hill. When we came to get him, he was missing. I don't know why they buried him twice. I think it was because the village people wanted him in a churchyard where a priest of some sort read a prayer over him. I was going home to the States, but I found your address in his belongings. I knew you'd want to find him."

Bobby, this true friend, had traveled hundreds of miles to bring me here. We were not finished with our journey.

June 10. Bobby and I set out by jeep for the long trip to Ulm. In the little town of Reutti, just out of Ulm, we found the (American) cemetery. Now the fact of death hit me as never before. The lieutenant in charge consulted some records. "Yes, we put him in Plot D." Oh, God, that was it. Up till now I had subconsciously refused to accept that fact. But a few minutes later I stood closer to my Charles than I had for two years.

His dog tag was nailed to a small white cross. This was a bleak, unbeautiful place. It brought such a moment of sorrow that I can hardly write it here. To know that my brother lay dead in German soil! I hesitate to record it here, what I believe to be a fact—that a part of the cemetery was under black crosses, black for the German enemy. Did I imagine that? It seemed too inhuman to have happened, even that close to the war memories. What I remember still better was the subdued kindness of the German villagers once they knew I had come a long way to find a dead brother, and would go on farther. But standing in the graveyard over the cross with his name tacked on, I did not feel at all dramatic. When Bobby wasn't looking I simulated a hand salute.

I didn't accomplish the mission of moving his body out of Germany. Yet he lay under an American flag with many other American boys. God bless his dear memory.

*   *   *

The above part of the personal journal was difficult to read after many years. It was written in pencil at night whenever we slept, sometimes in military barracks, sometimes in commercial hotels of the towns. During the long drive back to Paris where I could use my orders to take us both back to Britain by plane, I questioned Bobby at length about my brother's last days. I supplemented these talks by questioning another American, an Army transport pilot from Baltimore, Cooper Walker. He had spent a last leave in Paris with Charles and Bobby. Walker extended the substance of what Bobby Fenwick told me, which was something like this:

"In the final days and weeks of his life, Charles wasn't his usual self. His cheerfulness was there, but forced."

"I had the strangest feeling about him," continued Walker. "The war was almost over, and he'd been in some of its roughest parts. He didn't say so, but the impression I got was that he didn't expect to make it home. He wasn't all morbid. We three had a big time in Paris. We put on a real farewell party. But—it's strange—when I later heard that Charles was killed, I wasn't surprised."

I carried Charles's leatherbound diary for the next month or so, never opened it, and returned it by hand to his widow. Perhaps it was not intended that I learn anything about life from the death of others. I was no wiser than the wisest thinker. We on earth can do more than observe and speculate as to ultimate meanings. I would hang on to the conviction that the free will which some of us are allowed is a very precious belonging. If by taking thought and action, we can order our lives only by an iota, that is what we should do. It is certain that much in life is difficult, but neither is anything impossible to the human will.

*   *   *

Personal Journal

July 3 (1945). Aboard the Queen Mary at Greeneck in the Firth of Clyde. Yesterday at 1130 hours we left Attlebridge by truck for Norwich, there entrained for Scotland. At 1630 hours this morning we detrained and came on board. Thus a circle is about to close as on Friday I am homeward bound on the same great ship which brought me over. How terribly different this homecoming will be without Charles. What will it be for mother and daddy, broken and older. But there will be my darling Mary and my lovely kids.

July 8. HOMEWARD BOUND. Yesterday the big ship began to vibrate and to stir. We were under way. Oh, what a flood of feelings to the heart—home! home! home! God, I have more than I deserve. The Lord has been my shepherd.

6.

My Three Mentors

"DON'T PRESS ME," said my father from the head of the Sunday family dinner table.

He was responding to my ill-considered remark "Sort of sad President Roosevelt didn't live to enjoy V-E day, don't you think, sir?"

It was a normal attitude on my part. I was still in uniform and on order to proceed to the Pacific theater after two weeks of R & R. I remembered the early morning shock when my roommate at Division headquarters came charging in from his shower.

"Hey, does it take the President's death to get you out of the sack?"

I leaped from bed. "How's that again?"

"It's on the radio. He's dead."

"Oh—terrible."

No soldier could have felt otherwise, but there was a different feeling in my parents' privileged but nerve-wracked home. The head of the family was standing, the better to carve the large succulent turkey, an act he performed with skill and pleasure. A butler waited to pass each plate. Two maids followed with assortments of gravy, cranberry sauce, summer vegetables. It was a feast for my homecoming. Down each side of the ornate refectory board ranged the five handsome grandchildren and two pretty daughters-in-law. At the table's foot sat the host's adoring, authoritative, opinionated wife, long-tormented by pride and prejudice.

We had all trooped in here along the red carpeted hallway from the clubby library, with its rich leather, varnished furniture and red brick fireplace. There were floor-to-ceiling bookshelves, fine sets of the master writers and few best sellers. No junk admitted here, unless it was a section of green-and-crimson bound typescripts of my published books and magazine pieces, each volume marked Merrie Christmas with date. I'd solved the difficulty of finding gifts for the wealthy by giving my mother the present only I could produce. We elders took predinner cocktails, the youngsters had soft drinks, while we shared family and public news before marching to the dining room.

"Don't press me," my father had answered, and I felt annoyed at myself. Of course, I had not forgotten the grave I'd stood beside in Germany, nor the chair that wasn't at the festive table. Without holding Charles apart from some 300,000 battle deaths of World War II, I should have known that every killed-in-action son is special.

But Charles's own home, his bereaved widow and two children, seemed hardly considered here. I had given the unopened diary to the widow. She had wept in my arms, and sobbed pathetic words, "You know I just couldn't do this with your father or mother."

How little I understood the underlying torrent of emotions that surged here. My gentle mother, growing up with small town religious prejudice, had opposed Charles's match to his dark beauty, before, during and after the marriage. Incredibly, she had cried out, "I don't want any Catholic grandchildren," and my straight-arrow Mary said, "You should thank God for any kind."

At the outdoor wedding ceremony (neither the Episcopal nor Catholic parish was tolerant of mixed marriages, and the bride's cousins were forbidden to act as attendants) my mother who came heavily tranquilized became tipsy with champagne. I saw Charles go and kiss her when many were pretending not to notice. My father, such a stalwart in every crisis, had taken to his bed and did not come to the wedding of his namesake and business heir-apparent. There was the usual merry making of a nuptial feast, but there was an underflow of ill-will and unhappiness among the family elders of both sides. These recollections came back to me when I was home from that German site of the

American military cemetery and I unwillingly began to understand that Charles hadn't much wanted to come back. What I
didn't comprehend until I wrote about it, an emotional purge of
a novel, years afterwards, was the riptide of submerged ani-
mosity and tormented conscience of the parental household. My
father's loathing of Roosevelt was cruelly exacerbated by the
battlefield death which came closest.

For myself, I had until the war taken little notice of national
politics, beguiled as I was by local and historical doings, but I had
now been crowded by the incentive to do some thinking. Some
observers of running events, with whom I had acquaintance and
admiration, H.L. Mencken and Charles A. Beard, were early in
concluding that FDR's cure for the depression had a counterpart. If Mencken and Beard were right, the American President
and the German Chancellor chose a common solution for their
problems. It was war.

Mencken I came to know, after some years of worship from a
distance, in the 1930s, when he took an interest in my biogra-
phies and other writings. Shortly after Roosevelt's reelection in
1936, Mencken wrote and invited me to lunch alone with him in
his Hollins street home. A male servant brought us boiled
chicken with a Rhine wine and beer, while I listened to the sage
expound on many subjects—poetry, books, publishers and politics. I chiefly remember one pronouncement:

"If there isn't a war by the next election, 1940, Roosevelt will
start one. He will never be an ex-president. He'll die in office like
a king."

Shortly after that luncheon, I met historian Charles A. Beard.
This tall, eagle-visaged, gentle-mannered scholar was giving a
series of lectures at Johns Hopkins University. His subject one
day was the early American presidents and when he reached the
eighth of these, Beard departed from his script to say, "I go with
some trepidation into President Martin Van Buren, because I've
been told that the latest and best biographer is in the audience."

This was catnip to a young author. After the lecture I went
forward and introduced myself. It was the beginning of a warm
friendship, indeed a discipleship. Beard invited me to bring my

wife and dine with him next day at the faculty club. We exchanged compliments as friendly authors do. He came up with a line from my Van Buren book where Little Van was described as one "who rowed to his objects on muffled oars." Actually, it was a quoted passage from John Randolph of Roanoke, and I had made it the theme and judgment of my biography. In turn, I marvelled at Beard's fluid prose in his numerous histories and essays. He answered, "Well, I wrestle and revise each sentence and paragraph, and finally have to let them pass—only wishing I could have done better."

Our conversation flowed like a love scene, time out of mind, until an undergraduate appeared to remind Beard that he was overdue at an evening seminar. In many subsequent meetings—too few as I look back—he would repeatedly say, "I don't want my son to die for the sands of Egypt." He foresaw, as Mencken did, that Roosevelt was intent on joining a war that was not in the American interest.

Since I was then trying for an army commission, I said as much and little more. Beard never commented on or attempted to alter my contradictory desire for military service, much as I opposed our entrance into the struggle. He aimed at bigger targets, public opinion which he reached through his contemporary writings and Congressional committees. He testified against the draft, Lend Lease, the destroyers given to Britain and the forbidden Third Term.

Beard and I had a friend in common at *Harper's* magazine, George Leighton, who later edited a biography of Beard. Leighton wrote: "He became an attorney with his country as his client."

In the decade 1935-46, Beard laid down a heavy barrage against Roosevelt, in articles, testimony and books, first to prevent his joining the war, and then to condemn him for it. A summary reads:

> Confronted by the difficulties of a deepening domestic crisis
> and the comparative ease of a foreign war, what will President
> Roosevelt do? . . . he will choose the latter . . . plunge the country
> into a European war, when it comes, far more quickly than did

President Wilson. . . . His sympathies are so well known as to need no documentation. . . . [He is supported by] Stalinists who are bent on "saving Russian democracy." [Beard quoted the fourth act of Henry IV] . . . "Therefore, my Harry, be it thy course to busy giddy minds with foreign quarrels". . . . I propose that Congress reject his bill with such force that no President of the United States will ever dare again [attempt] to suspend the Constitution and . . . confer upon himself limitless dictatorial powers over life and death . . . leaving us with a stupendous debt, a large and sprawling military establishment . . . confronted with a Russian despotism . . . its zealous followers in every country on earth, our own included. . . . this is what our imperialistic internationalist adventure has brought us.

Though Beard and I corresponded during the war, I did not see him again for some eight years after Pearl Harbor. I was then a Washington-based syndicated columnist; he a feeble old man under the liberal establishment's whiplash of post-war internationalism.

Secondary writers were anti-Roosevelt on World War II, and suffered accordingly. Beard alone among these unfortunates was a foremost man of letters in the English-speaking world. His classic narrative histories through the 1920s and '30s were published by Macmillan, Scribners, Harpers, Knopf, Oxford, Rinehart and other lordly houses. But the Beard books of 1945 and 1948 that examined the Roosevelt foreign policies did not make publishers row. They were driven back to the campus university presses. His reviewers, once from the top drawer, looked away.

Later still, when Beard was in his mid-seventies and nearing his end, some of his loyalists rallied to put out a biographical anthology. They ran into trouble. Some of Beard's old friends would not speak to him; others declined invitations to contribute chapters to his biography. Before enough could be persuaded, Charles Beard died. The book about him did not find a metropolitan publisher; it was brought out by the University of Kentucky Press, though Beard's academic connections were De Pauw, Columbia, Oxford and Johns Hopkins. The man whose books sold 11,353,163 copies, not counting publications in Japanese, German and Braille, found himself at the hands of the "book-burners." Publishers, critics, government custodians of important documents, ex-friends seemed bent on destroying his works and name by studied neglect. They gave him what John Chamberlain called the Averted Gaze.

Howard K. Beale, editor of *Charles A. Beard: An Appraisal* (1954), tells in his introduction what he came up against in collecting the dozen writers and their input to Beard's biography: "Some men who had loved Beard came to dislike him bitterly. . . . The participants lost interest. . . . Two of us drew up a suggested list of contributors and subjects. The various interested people were invited to luncheon at the Princeton Club of New York. Some of those invited expressed such dislike of what Beard stood for that they would have nothing to do with a project to honor him. . . . Some of them, once friends of Beard, had come to hate what he stood for. Others who still cherished the old affections were too completely out of sympathy to say kind things and did not want to say harsh ones."

Somehow, though it had been planned as a presentation on the old scholar's 73rd and then his 74th birthday, the book appeared as a memorial six years after his death. It went largely unnoticed, as did *The Making of Charles A. Beard* (1955) by his widow and once-collaborator, which had to be published by a vanity house.

Whatever the merit or demerit of Beard's ideology, this elder statesman of letters had earned a right to be heard. The American people's right to hear him is imbedded in the Bill of Rights. Beard was in full command of his wits and erudition.

His general indictments, always backed by a bill of particulars, were logical extensions of his massive historical knowledge. He believed that Roosevelt's ambition, in an age of Titans—Stalin, Hitler, Churchill, de Gaulle and Asian leaders not yet to the fore—extended to making himself chief executive of world government. This would automatically require the ingestion of the American democratic republic. Beard never held views that the "decline of the West" was inevitable and scheduled by fate. Rather, he felt the Republic had suffered from avoidable mistakes which he enumerated: (1) listening to 19th-century leaders who wanted "more of the world" and to 20th-century presidents who wanted "to save the world;" (2) misdefining "major power" as a nation with many allies and overseas investments, instead of one with the resources for self-sufficiency. As Beard neared death and afterwards, he experienced the legendary treatment of a bad-news messenger.

Late learner and superficial thinker as I surely was, I could not absorb the meanings of global events while I rested and recuperated on my North American farm, so blessedly separated from the chaotic continents of Europe and Asia.

In time, I would understand that the vaunted American independence had been compromised by interventions and continuing involvements in faraway lands. And I would come to see that the intellectual persecution, for their opinions, of non-conformists like Beard, was integral to the awful and ironic aftermath of our sweeping World War II victories.

7.

Normalcy and Peace

SWEET MEADOWS FARM, where Mary and I lived and raised our children, was some 200 acres of moist grassland under a hill, watered by two streams and an icy spring which supplied the house. The layout was ideal for pasturing beef cattle and boarding brood mares, its chief enterprise. The frame homestead was white, red-chimneyed at each end and was reached from the country road by a white-sand driveway which followed the bending contours of a vanished wagon trail. We had built on the site of a fallen farmhouse of long ago. The atmosphere was one of continuous livability. Its well-stocked library had been accumulated from Princeton, Cambridge and Baltimore book stores.

In August 1945 I returned to find my pastures unkempt, fences down and a general air of disarray. I had bargained with a neighbor to run his stock, cut the hay, and generally use the fields as his own, but he had been careless with what was mine.

However, this three-year look of disuse brought me unexpected wartime reparations, some wages of the winner, paid in kind, the droit de vanquereur. I learned that the polo field of the nearby Pikesville Armory had been converted to a POW stockade. Hundreds of German captives were available as farm labor for no more than "cigarette money." I called on the commandant, an old friend of the hunting field, Major Goss Stryker, and he ordered several truckloads of subdued Huns to Sweet Meadows Farm.

The POWs went through the fields like locusts, scything the grass and overgrowth, heaping and burning trash, sinking fence posts and nailing planks. They were obviously relieved to be out of confinement for several days and to earn the minimal stipend.

Army regulations required American officers on leave to stay in uniform, and I found no more hostility among these Nordic fieldhands than I had encountered at that far-off German churchyard. One afternoon a sudden thunderstorm swept the farm and we all stampeded for shelter in the hay barracks. There at close quarters I felt less comfortable than at large in the fields. Some of the captives pointed to my Air crew wings, saying "Fleigerkorps?"

When I assented there followed a barrage of questions. I heard place names of German cities which had been B-24 targets. Had they bombed this one? That one? The quizzing had a pathetic tone as if these men were only asking if I had visited their hóme towns and seen their folks.

In contrast to future veterans, World War II soldiers luxuriated in what a later generation would call an ego trip. Mine was a deluxe passage, not just with family and friends; old acquaintances at the grocery and filling station made me glad I had gone and come back.

Dinners at the Hunt Club, cocktail parties in friendly homes were the order of the occasion. The State Guard, in which I had not earned so much as a private first class stripe, turned out a formation at the Armory, where I proudly trooped the line. I took my sons to see the Orioles play International League baseball (big league was not yet for Baltimore), and the gatekeeper waved us in free because of my uniform.

But in all this there was an irritating rub. After living amid English austerity, I saw little evidence that America had been at war, in fact, was still engaged in the Far East. The drab garments of British women had been an accustomed sight, and the memory seemed to rebuke the colorful and daring dressing all about me.

Military vehicles predominated in Britain, but Maryland highways buzzed with private cars. When I inquired about gasoline rationing, I learned that practically everybody with a bungalow was rated as a farmer and drew agricultural allowances. I was a guest of a horse owner at Delaware Park Race Track, a hundred miles away. Not only owners, trainers and jockeys were grouped in the farm population, so also were the sleek thoroughbred racers which didn't live on hay alone.

Hardships our European allies and enemies had borne were not shared by Americans, that was plain. Our country seemingly had no awareness of world realities.

True, there were families bereaved, and families sweating out the Pacific War, but it was impossible not to wonder what would happen if this happy land were put to the test. We returnees had seen British villages stripped by severe economies, and heaps of rubble in vacant lots. In France and Germany, we had seen the broken cities, smashed bridges, rutted fields. Four decades later, in the 1980s, I still wondered how America would react to direct attack and invasion.

Not all the homecoming was joyous. One evening, taking highballs on the lawn with my wife, I was hit in the nape of the neck by a pailful of water. From the upstairs porch I heard a scampering of feet and mischievous giggles. The children had done this trick—I thought—to send a message of unwelcome. "Go away, Yank," it seemed to tell me. Beneath the semblance of "welcome home" was childish resentment of the strange man who now usurped their mother's attention. How trifling it seems in retrospect, but I felt deeply hurt at the time.

Then there was a lavish cocktail affair given by my surviving brother. He had stayed out of military service on grounds of a nervous affliction and married a wealthy neighbor during wartime. We two were nothing alike. Our upbringings were at the extremes. Mine took place when the family was small town and merely well-off; his, when riches had enormously increased.

Mary and I, the guests of honor at this brother's party and the last to depart, were about to do so, when he sentimentally proposed a final drink. I surmised that he had something personal to tell me. Our bond was that we both loved Charles. Would this draw us closer together? I hoped with all my heart that it would. The terrible undertow of prejudice, sorrow and political hatred in my parents' home tugged at me. More than anything, that night, waiting for my brother to speak, I hoped for words of fraternal love between us. But what he said, in the form of an insinuating question, pierced me with resentful anger. He asked, "Was Charles going to get a divorce when he came home?"

The nasty implication was unmistakable. My mind flashed back to other hints that Charles felt he wasn't going to make it back, didn't much want to do so, and had died an unhappy man. Was all that in that diary which I'd brought unopened? These thoughts surged through me. I rose and blurted my anger at the brother who sat there, smirking at this sadistic coup.

Mary, her instincts always subtle and quick, tugged my elbow. We abruptly left. "Don't you see?" she said as we drove off. "He's the brother who didn't go to war. He wanted you to think about what often happens when wives are left behind." It was the fiendish Iago touch, the stolen handkerchief, the planted suspicion. "A pot marred in the making," Mary added elliptically.

I understood the remark well enough. She meant that this surviving brother was the product of parental mismangement which had changed him from a spoiled rich kid to a vindictive man.

It would be another twenty years before I translated the far-from-unusual plot into a novel. I found a tag of verse that expressed my theme, "There is thy gold," said Romeo to the apothecary who sold him the death-drug. "Worse poison to men's souls."

My novel was about the ruinous power of wealth to corrupt those who don't know how to handle it. It was about greed of wealthy men who married and/or inherited their money. In the years ahead when my father had died and my mother lay in total paralysis, I wrote *West of Washington* (1962) which purged my bewilderment.

Only Mary knew that I worked with hot tears on my face. She encouraged me to untangle the knot, and there were those who told me, "Bravo." But the novel cost me more friends than it held. It also provided the comic scramble to follow Mrs. Grundy in scandalized disapproval. I watched with amusement the natural selection of fair-weather friends from the other kind.

At the 1945 homecoming, however, too much was going on to allow unhappy matters to poison the atmosphere of this R & R interlude. My parents (not exactly farmers but well-supplied with gasoline coupons) drove off for their late summer vacation at the Homestead, Hot Springs, Virginia. In the Sweet Meadows library I would think about my interrupted writing life. Two or more pieces made publication. More immediately I thought of how to find a salaried job after returning from the Orient.

The Government feared unemployment, and we had been given many job-hunting lectures before leaving the ETO. I composed a list of options, somewhat as follows:

There were family insurance business branch offices in Clarksburg and Charles Town. I had sentimental leanings toward these pleasant towns, one in the Allegheny Mountains, one in the Shenandoah Valley. But I had never been a businessman and did not relish the prospect. The Air Corps had vaguely proposed that I stay on as an instructor, which included an automatic promotion, but it meant being often away from home. I had a yen to return to schoolteaching, but it paid poorly. I had written a lot for the *Baltimore Sun-Papers* and might logically apply for a job. Another opportunity tempted me above all else. I told my wife, "I hear there's an opening to be stable master and assistant whip at the Hunt Club. That way I could be with horses and hounds. I could live the outdoor life, and write on the side."

"Do it," she said without much zest." "If you're sure it's what you want."

I had never had enough cross-country riding, and the chance seemed too good to miss. I picked up the phone and called the Master of Hounds, Stuart Janney, an old friend, recently back from service in the Marine Corps. He said the job was open, and mine for the taking. Hadn't we better talk it over? Next evening the MFH sat me down in his parlor for a drink and he fondly presented my 10-year-old son who accompanied me with a handsome pair of hunting boots.

"There are two things you won't like about this job," Janney said. "One is that several times a year, we destroy a horse that's getting old or has broken down. We feed him to the hounds. I can't see you for that work."

"What else?" I weakly asked.

"The pay isn't much." He named it. Even with what I could expect to make as a freelance writer, I saw the proposition fading into unreality. Janney seemed relieved (he eventually engaged a better man), but not half so much as Mary.

As the next best choice I phoned for an engagement with the *Sun-Papers*. In the outer office I encountered the portly Mencken and the equally well-fleshed Moko Yardley, the newspaper's cartoonist. The latter greeted me warmly, saying, "Why Henry, you remember Holmes?"

The great iconoclast stared in mock dismay at my beribboned uniform and conditioned figure. "Of course, I know Holmes but not in that shape." We shook hands. "You'll have to work up a respectable bay window."

He patted his own. The *Sun-Papers* had benched him, their heaviest editorial hitter who'd been outrageously anti-Roosevelt and anti-war. He had used the interim to write his memoirs. Now, like myself, he wanted a place here. He'd have no trouble about that, but it would be the last of him.

I would see Mencken at the three political Conventions of '48, writing so furiously under the hot new television lights that would cause his fatal stroke. But he'd reveled at Philadelphia, particularly in his torment of the big simpleton, Henry Wallace, Progressive Party candidate. One of Mencken's happiest sallies, which backfired, though he intended a compliment by it, was in an article where he congratulated a swinging orator "the color of a good 10 cent cigar." I remember going down on the floor to learn by interview how the jest went over. A dignified Afro deacon growled at me, "I'd like to sock that fella on the snout."

But Mencken, almost alone that year, picked Truman to whip Dewey. At a mint julep stag party, we asked him why.

"Just because Truman's the bigger boob," he told us.

Wishing, like every other journalist, for a wit like Mencken's, I went in to see Neil Swanson, the chief editor. I asked for a reporting job, the ground-level beginning. He grumbled that published authors only signed on as reporters between their books. But "probably" he would take me on if I could show up for work the Tuesday after Labor Day. In view of my orders to the Far East, this offer seemed no better than a brush-off, but I thanked him and went my way. In the corridor I encountered another newspaper friend, R. P. Harriss, the book editor. He exclaimed, "My God, have you heard? We've dropped a uranium bomb on Japan."

Of blockbusters, fire bombs, delayed action bombs that penetrated buildings before exploding, incendiary bombs that were laid by night and took fire in grain fields when the sun came up, I had heard. A uranium bomb, no. The new-fangled weapon did not intrigue me. But when I stopped at the post office to pick up the mail, another chance informant told me more. The radio had reported the total destruction of a Japanese city, Hiroshima, with several thousand enemy casualties.

"How perfectly ghastly," he exclaimed.

I wasn't at all horrified. A big death toll on the sneak attackers of Pearl Harbor served 'em right, I thought. Besides, I had several good friends in the Pacific theater. Their assault on the main islands would be helped by aerial mauling of the defenders. Then came the second bomb on Nagasaki. World War II had ended in victory. With a minimum of red tape I was officially "separated" from the Army at nearby Fort Meade.

Astonishingly, on the Tuesday after Labor Day '45, I became a newspaperman, a *Baltimore Sun* reporter in what had been called "normalcy." It was a brief but wonderful time of my life. I was writing daily about mundane affairs of courthouse politics and other crimes, local education and industry in the mightiest nation on earth.

There never had been such a country-with-a-conscience. We were converting our military power into immense prosperity. Congress was sharing our good fortune with the luckless and helpless people of our common world. Joy was it in that day to be alive, I would paraphrase Wordsworth, and to be aged 39 was very heaven.

8.

A Study in the Will to Win

WRITERS WRITE BY COMPULSION. They wrote before there were typewriters, fountain pens, before there was a printing press; they have written with wooden sticks and stone chisels, have stored their compositions in memory to be passed down in folklore. They even write with scant audience or recompense.

But I think most writers like to have an outside person for a mentor. Fitzgerald and Wolfe institutionalized the editor-mentor in Maxwell Perkins. My pre-war editor-mentor at Harper Brothers was Eugene Saxton, but he died while I was overseas. I was pleased to get a letter from Cass Canfield, editor at the House of Harper, asking if I had a book in mind. He proposed I come to the Century Club, New York City, for a discussion. I showed the letter to the *Sun's* city editor and asked for a mid-week day off, saying I would make it up.

"You bet," he said, and added, "If you've got bigger ideas, for God's sake, don't let anything around here stand in your way."

My ideas weren't large. I took to newspapering like a duck to the mill pond. I was attached to Sweet Meadows farm, had acquired three horses as gifts (they were broken-down racers), was foxhunting with my two sons, Hunter and Peter, every Saturday, and I padded my salary with some magazine sales. I was content to live with Mary in this cradle of comfort. Or so I thought.

At the Century Club where Canfield turned me over to William Briggs, long-time Harper editor, I learned that what was wanted from me was a companion book to go with my *Lives* of Van Buren and Burr. Harper's would reprint these by a new photographic method provided we decided on a third subject. It was tempting. We went through many nominees—Hamilton, favored—but I warmed to none. In truth, I did not want to do another costume biography. I wanted to do creative work.

It need not be fiction, but something out of the war experience which was very real to me. The reality was intensified by recent thinking brought on by observation and reading. I went home, promising to work out something. It was already taking shape in my mind and notes.

Strangely, the stirrings did not relate to military adventure. They had to do with the Elbe river episode, with what I'd seen of the complacent home front and my father's once-removed memories of Reconstruction when an area of America had been invaded, defeated and subjugated. I paid a visit to relatives in Charles Town, where I'd spent some boyhood summers. I recalled that time when many Confederate veterans were at large. I remembered their bitter warning, often repeated, "Son, don't ever lose a war."

This inspiration had turned into a premonition, and there were other sources. One was a nagging dissatisfaction, to be in midlife without much accomplishment. Another was the memory of being in Europe on the sad mission with Bobby Fenwick. Several times we crossed, by field ambulance and jeep, the pontoon bridges and other landmarks that separated France and Germany. We had jokingly agreed that we needed no roadmarkers on frontier posts to tell France from Germany. One of these devasted nations was struggling to its feet; the other was waiting to be helped up. In German fields, although the season was past planting time, there would be men and women turning the soil for late crops. Sometimes they used hand utensils; often their ploughs were drawn by a milkcow since draft animals were confiscated. By contrast, the French fields were apt to be abandoned, though the haystacks and sheds were occupied by merry jug-drinkers and amorous couples. Both countries had been defeated, but the Germans after fierce resistance; France by early capitulation.

"Never lose a war!"

Very faintly (since I was reporting only Maryland news), some intimations reached me that America was already losing one on several fronts. At the Atomic Energy Laboratory in New Mexico, Russian spies were afoot and American turncoats on the loose. At the Potsdam Conference, the new president, Truman, had been unable to reverse Roosevelt's concessions to Stalin at Yalta. Dire results were showing in East Europe. Charles Beard's penetrative writings, now my must-reading, suggested to me that the rogue-word "isolationist" had the basic synonym of "nationalist." I thought that excessive internationalism could easily slide into non-nationalism, non-Americanism, and anti-Americanism; that foreign aid could become a share-the-wealth folly, a form of tribute to buy friendship and peace-on-earth. My cynicism about politics underwent a chain reaction. I marked two passages, one from Mencken, one from Beard:

> "Even in a great Depression few if any starve, and even in a great war the number who suffer by it is vastly surpassed by the number who fatten on it and enjoy it." *(Beard)*

> "For many years the imperialists and internationalists have been asserting that the United States is a great power and must assume the responsibilities of a great power. Of course the United States is a great power, and will be until it has exhausted its coal, oil and iron, and the morale of its people has degenerated with the exhaustion of economic opportunities at home." *(A Mencken Chrestomathy)*

All this rudderless cognitation was taking me toward ill-defined forebodings. America might have to fight again in my generation, or my children's. Some future defeat was no more impossible than what had happened to France, Germany and the Southern Confederacy. Into my head jumped the familiar Kipling lines:

> "If you can meet with triumph and disaster
> And treat those two imposters just the same."

Americanize that couplet, and it says something about national determination to become a complete and mature nation. Kipling gave me a working title, *Those Two Imposters*. I would examine the phenomenon of success-and-failure, victory-and-defeat, as related to persons and peoples, to societies and sovereign nations.

We all know that much, if not most, personal failure is self-inflicted, by laziness, dissipation, instant or prolonged suicide. And this could happen to America, I thought. Something strange had darkened the nation's hours of triumph over the Axis—something that pertained, at first, to the A-bomb.

By all that seemed right and logical, Captain Truman of Battery D had wisely treated this then-ultimate weapon as a greater artillery shell. Its use spared hundreds of thousands of American lives, not to mention Japanese. Thus, our joy should be unalloyed over the incineration of Hiroshima and Nagasaki. Yet it was not.

As I read the high-calibre writing that resulted from the products of the Los Alamos Laboratory and similar workshops, I recognized the virus of guilt. It was in startling contrast to the uninhibited rejoicing when we put down the Nazi enemy. Something had gone wrong.

As early as September '45, a Soviet defector, Igor Gouzenko, confessed in Canada that Russian agents had been stealing our atomic data for more than two years. Never forgetting the Elbe River incident of our forced-down plane, I was not surprised, but indignant. It seemed enough (and there must be much more not yet publicly known) to anger the American people, perhaps to the extent of demanding a diplomatic break with the USSR.

Instead of enraging the country, the Soviet perfidy fed our sense of wrongdoing in ourselves. Nothing is more productive of failures, and often of self-destruction, than this guilt complex. Later, a member of the technical staff at the Oak Ridge Laboratory, Medford Evans, told in his book, *The Secret War For The A-Bomb*, what had happened at the news of Hiroshima. Of the 75,000 employees, the large majority ". . . rejoiced and looked at each other with pride. Their husbands, brothers and sons would be coming home sooner and alive. The war would end at once and in victory. Their country would now lead and guarantee a decent world."

But a minority of about 500, Evans wrote, expressed shock and dismay. In some small cadre of the population, I judged, the guilt infection had set in. This was not the first time it had happened to us. The Abolitionists of the North were the core of the protest against slavery in our country that proclaimed freedom. Many high-minded persons in the South flinched at dismembering the Union by secession. Such sensitivity as displayed about the A-bomb was well taken if applied solely to humane aspects, but it is not an attitude that wins national wars as Truman well understood.

And what if, as suspicion went around, this self-blame had been "engineered" by the Soviet enemy. If so, it would be a tactic to "denature" the weapon, James Burnham wrote, a warlike method of "spiking our guns." It could be the psychological means of planting self-destructive tendencies in the American mind, such as unilateral disarmament.

By propagandizing a working minority in the United States, the enemy was reaching for the jugular. I was coming to a set of conclusions about the state of our Union, and had reached an impasse of how to write my projected book without pontificating. There was no point in declaring American virtue as supreme in a wicked world. The law of nations does not provide that righteousness must prevail. I could not assume that wrong would fall by the wayside. I must narrow my scope and zero in on a target of affirmation—victory. This concept perfectly matched the American worship of accomplishment. Never lose a war—never accept failure—fight to win—work to succeed. In the opening paragraph of my book I drew a bead on this theme:

English-speaking peoples (I wrote) readily understand the concepts of personal success and failure. In the Mediterranean world and in the Orient, ambitions of men and women are turned toward the abstract. Passion and philosophy, intrigue and revenge, spin the life-plots south of the Rio Grande and the Pyrenees and east of Gibraltar. In North America there is candid materialism, like it or not. A man who competes at all in the games of life is marked, by himself and by others, as a success or failure.

I went on to stress this well-recognized American distinction, this contrast between success and failure. I said never mind "moral victory" and "spiritual triumph," for in wartime they will

count for nothing. So, I wrote, let us not seek refuge in figura-
tive or poetic double talk. By success I meant the attainment of a
designated goal. By failure I meant the harsh and brutal fact of
defeat. We could learn (I wrote) something about this subject by
a study of great and memorable persons, provided they were
equal in courage and honor. Two names came to mind. One was
George Washington; the other Robert E. Lee. In the contest of
preserving our nation from an enemy assault, consider these two
men.

Each was an admired leader of a desperate American rebellion
against imposing odds. Writing in 1945-6, I did not have the
example of the Vietnam conflict to prove that wars are not always
won by the biggest battalions and deadliest weapons, but history
offered many examples of wars won by a leader, and his nation,
who simply will not accept defeat. Getting to specifics, no matter
what the humiliation for George Washington at Long Island, no
matter what the suffering at Valley Forge, no matter how many
years elapsed between the Declaration of Independence and the
Battle of Yorktown, no matter how often the French alliance
proved a delusion, Washington was a leader who did not recog-
nize unsuccess.

Wars are lost by a leader who is too much of a Noble Loser. If
he is defending an institution of which he disapproves (slavery),
if he does not really hate his enemy (the Federal Union), if he
can rationalize battlefield defeat as the "will of God" (the hand-
iest excuse known to man), this commander will never overcome
a determined foe, but will go down in gallant frustration as did
Lee.

I saw, in Generals Washington and Lee, the equation (or one of
many equations) for winning and losing. There was one passage
of my book which many reviewers quoted, some in derision:

> The treatment of the phenomenon of success and failure allows
> no pity or the lessons are lost. Both these great men accepted with
> supreme aplomb the lot that was theirs, and lived their remaining
> years without being either bloated or broken by what had
> transpired. . . .
> It would be beyond belief that the legends of George Wash-

ington and Robert E. Lee did not enter into the molding of the American character.

The times when this nation and this people have plunged forward to the taking of new territory, to the accumulation of wealth and a deeply-felt destiny—that was the spirit of Washington. But when our nation and its people have confronted an enemy with anything less than the will to annihilate him, when they have yearned and haggled for peace instead of victory, when they looked for alibis in some right-or-wrong argument, or a dodge into the imagined will of God—that was the spirit of Lee, gentlemanly Loser.

Of course, I could not foresee in the late 1940s that a time was not far off when we no longer won our wars. The book, eventually titled *Washington and Lee: A Study in the Will to Win,* was rejected at Harpers and had to wait 20 years for publication (1966), when its time had come. Much would happen to America in the decades of 1950-60-70. I believe that the deathbed scenes of my exemplary heroes tell a lot about current American history.

Lee, 64, refused the medicine that his doctors pressed upon him to prolong his life. Washington, 67, submitted to blistering and bleeding by three bedside physicians, and grimly declared: "Doctor, I die hard. . . . "

Both men were authentic heroes. But Lee was a gentleman who could not win; Washington was a leader who would not lose. The American future would depend on which sorts of leaders were chosen—compulsive winners or plausible losers.

Over the next three decades as a Washington columnist with many trips abroad, I found nothing to change my mind. I did find much to encourage an enemy. It was everyday knowledge that many in our population did not love America, did not want this country to survive and win, or simply did not care. My writings, here and elsewhere, never addressed this group. I addressed their opposite numbers who care very much.

Despite America's past sins against humanity—the slaughter of Indians, the enslavement of Blacks—and despite the materialism of the free enterprise system and the grossness of politics, there is no sound case for losing any war, just or unjust. Defeat by battle or blackmail would destroy the great good that is resident here.

9.

Never Lose A War

ALL ROADS LED ME TO WASHINGTON, the watchtower of world history. By Christmastime 1946 I was no longer a reporter, but a columnist, and three months later I was nationally syndicated. It happened in rapid steps, but not a pounce. It involved my leaving the security of two excellent jobs for the chancy career of a freelancer. Tipped off that the Kiplinger News Agency was starting a new magazine and scouting for writers, I drove over with Mary one Saturday for cocktails with John Denson, the hiring officer, and wife. A few days later I was invited back to meet Willard Kiplinger, legendary publisher of the Kiplinger Letters For Businessmen. We instantly struck it off. He offered me a staff editorship on the projected magazine, a generous salary, indication of prompt promotion; in all, a deal very difficult to refuse.

Had the *Sun-Papers* met my suggestion of matching the Kiplinger wage offer, I would have remained in Baltimore and on my farm, a parttime book writer. But the Washington salary was munificent by Baltimore newspaper standards, and there was an organizational fight in progress between the *Sun* and the *Guild.* I gave notice; I stayed on through the elections of November 1946, which produced in Maryland a new U.S. Senator and Governor, and in Washington the long-remembered 80th Congress. Around Thanksgiving I began commuting to the brick building on Northwest G Street, opposite the YMCA where Lyndon Johnson's aide, Walter Jenkins, would fall from grace in a homosexual arrest.

Willard Kiplinger, tall, gray, puckish, had a shrewdness which

54

he concealed under a hood of seeming insouciance. His editorial talent was for sensing and answering what the average American wanted to know about government—from the New Deal alphabetics to global complexities. My new boss ("Call me Kip") had devised a folksy, clippish style for answers and predictions. The first-class stamped Kiplinger Letters were personally addressed to subscribers, signed by himself. They sold like buttered popcorn through the midland states. When the war ended, Kip decided to repeat the success in magazine format for the same clientele. He wanted a unique product, as little as possible like *Barrons*, *Fortune*, *Business Week*, *Nation's Business* and the *Wall Street Journal*—but indispensable.

With no formula in mind, Kip raided other publications—*Life*, *Fortune*, *Newsweek*—for a professional staff. After a few briefings on his intent and policy, he withdrew supervision of the no-byline articles. He would pass judgment when the pioneer edition was in hand. Heads would roll, we well knew, if he was dissatisfied.

Trusting my luck, I guessed that a slice of entertainment about businessmen would balance the heavier fare. I shopped around Washington and came up with a yarn, "The Businessman's Lunch." I addressed every aspect in deadpan: weight-watching, favored dishes, comfortable decor, chummy companions and— the heart of the piece—dark, seductive nooks where tycoons and underlings could meet with secretaries and other extramarital intimates. I was holding my breath at the first editorial staff meeting when Willard Kiplinger read my anonymous story aloud to the group and exclaimed: "Now *there's* what we're after."

I did get another semi-spoof, based on a cross country plane trip to the major universities. It was not about education. It dealt with the subsidized amateurs who played college football, a practice not then commonplace or acknowledged. This caused an uproar among the coaches and alumni. I thought my job in jeopardy. We were an in-house publication, not the vehicle for exposé or satire. Some of my material was based on Ohio State University, my boss' alma mater, where his "disloyalty" was roundly denounced. Kip stood by my unsigned article in personal letters and a thumping editorial.

However, he did not care much for angering his readers. My next few pieces were safe interviews out of the Commerce and Treasury Departments. Then, again, I went for shock treatment. I profiled a construction engineer who had built most of the railroad bridges into Washington. Gradually, deep into the body of the piece, I revealed that he was Black. This was unusual in those days when Black professionals were mostly entertainers.

This article, coming from the home-and-hearth House of Kiplinger, jolted Middle America, but the publisher played it bland. He liked to move up front of the times—but not too far, not too fast. I later was entertained by the engineer when he was Governor of the Virgin Islands.

Meanwhile, I turned columnist in a small way. The owner of the weekly *Union News* in Towson, Maryland, stopped me on the street.

"When you go to Washington, how about sending back a regular newsletter on the affairs of state?"

"I wouldn't know enough about them."

"Well, don't take yourself too seriously. I'll pay you for trying."

We elevated "letter" to "column," and I commenced shortly before Christmas '46 to tell readers what little I knew about American public life. Before leaving for the new job, I had been propositioned by the county Boss, called Rolling Thunder, to run for an open seat in the House of Representatives with his endorsement. I declined, but kept a residual fondness for Rolling Thunder, and soon saw a chance to nationalize it. President Truman drew some criticism for attending the funeral of Boss Tom Pendergast in Missouri, at a time when Boss Hague of Jersey City was in trouble with the law. I did a column in favor of the vanishing race of public plunderers, the political bosshood, and gave it a patriotic ring. Whoever heard of a Boss who didn't love America? Or was a personally unattractive man? Or ever consorted with perverts? Or ever stole a boxcar? I likened Pendergast, Hague and the whole hierarchy back to Thurlow Weed to my own Boss whom I had loved when young.

Mary had slipped this column, and others, to a writer and public relationist, L.G. Shreve, who mailed the packet to McNaught Syndicate, Inc., New York City, distributor of Frank

R. Kent and numerous bestsellers on the editorial and comic pages. The Boss column caught on with the McNaught editors and I signed to a series of 10-year contracts that did not end until Ronald Reagan came to town.

For the rest of 1947, I worked for both Kiplinger and McNaught, dangerously serving two masters. But Kiplinger promoted me to Senior Staff Editor with a salary raise. Charlie MacAdams, the McNaught proprietor, sent me a bonus. The business articles were a nine-to-five routine, but the three-a-week column, later upped to five, had to be written after dark in the cheapest hotel room I could find, owing to the uncertainty of further employment. What sustained me in my ignorance and fatigue? Years later I looked back and gave the answer in some autobiographical musing.

"Partly it was the gift of gab. I might know nothing about the hard facts and the interior structure of the Federal Government and foreign affairs, but I was never without a strong opinion. My views were those of a tireless reader of history and biography, so that I brought into commentary a good deal of fundamental American philosophy. Partly, too, I stayed alive as a columnist on the conviction that a sentence, a paragraph, a unit of composition was no good if it did not 'sing' a little. The tune might be jaunty and sassy. It might be solemn or portentous. It must never be flat. The story it carried must never be dull. I was living on love—the love of writing."

In all honesty, I would not have been surprised at whatever outcome resulted from this sharply-personalized, highly-satirical outpouring. In time, I opposed the Marshall Plan, the Atlantic Alliance, reciprocal trade policies and everything not solidly pro-American. It was no strain on my part since I was writing my beliefs. If my offerings had been received with deafening silence, I could have concluded that they had no reader appeal. Had I got from McNaught Syndicate a reprimand and a threatened cancellation of contract, I would have withdrawn in disgust and defeat.

Instead, there came letters from all over the land where the columns were published on trial. For every batch that put down my nationalism as benighted reactionary nonsense, there were several batches that declared me a Daniel come to Judgment. Instead of go-slow signals from my Syndicate, I heard from Mildred Bellah, my New York editor, the regular admonitions of "keep up the good work."

I sought counsel on every hand by writing to the editors. "Be as contentious as possible," said one advisor. "Don't lose that satiric touch," said another. "Get a widespread appraisal of your work," said a third. I followed each suggestion. From the feedback I found a central reason for my acceptance as a commentator:

"Alexander: You're like a new girl come to town—a fresh face always attracts. You are the only war-generation conservative, a follow-on to David Lawrence, Ray Moley, Westbrook Pegler, George Sokolsky. You are a readable stylist, but not a deep-goer like Walter Lippman. Give us more news content."

This last comment was worrisome and valid. I did not know official Washington, and this had to be rectified. One day, an ex-Army officer phoned and said, "Alecks, I work for a trade association that has a tie-in with the *Worcester* [Mass.] *Telegram* which is a big user of your column. The editors don't really believe you're crazy, but they've asked me to check you out. How about having lunch?"

"Sure."

Good luck followed me like a faithful dog. At lunch, I was handed a key to Room 1391, National Press Building where the *Telegram* kept one of four desks. I could have it rent-free if I would feed in news bits about a new Representative from Massachusetts, Christian Herter, of whom great things were expected. I would see him become Eisenhower's Secretary of State and leave to become his State's Governor. I soon decided to pay my own rent and did so for the first year by ghost-editing a biography of John Nance Garner. I resigned from Kiplinger. I set out to go it alone and to know "everybody" in Washington. Over the years, I almost did.

As the town opened before me so did the whole world. All the military services, and most of the commercial lines (particularly the risky beginners), invited correspondents to ride their airplanes. I had only to put my finger on the map, and await "space available." By joining the Aviation Writers' Association and the

Travel Writers' Association, I soon had more travel invitations than I could accept. Till then I knew nothing of the world beyond North America and Western Europe, but during the next several years my columns were filed from all continents, planes aloft, ships at sea and submarines beneath.

By good fortune I arrived in Washington along with the men of destiny in the decades ahead. I was a freshman—and therefore on easy terms with other newcomers—with Jack and Bobby Kennedy, William Rogers and Richard Nixon, Stuart Symington, John Stennis, Lyndon Johnson and his garrulous brother Sam Houston Johnson, Paul Douglas, Hubert Humphrey, Everett Dirksen, Bill Fulbright, George Smathers, Bill Jenner, Joe McCarthy and many others.

I drew some cancellations. I made bloopers. One night I covered a press conference of the Hollywood Ten and proposed freeing them from the Black List. Fortunately, there was a Californian in the Syndicate office who knew these scriptwriters and attested to their communist ties. We killed the column.

Always digging for fresh material, I received from a friend at the *Baltimore Sun* (which declined the material) a packet of photostatted letters that showed Radio Commentator Fulton Lewis, Jr. in previous collaboration with Nazi Germans to make a separate peace. So dense was my ignorance that I had never heard of Lewis, a rightwing anti-Rooseveltor like myself, but I knew it was unlawful to dicker with a wartime enemy. Avid to sink my teeth into hard news, I wrote a three-column series and exposed Lewis (later a fast friend). The Syndicate axed the columns and asked me to think again.

"When you're better established, you can get into feuds with fellow journalists. It's too early."

I had many contacts at Johns Hopkins University, which produced Alger Hiss and Owen Lattimore. I met many intellectuals there and elsewhere who were enchanted by the One World concept. They regarded the "world" as more important than their country. They were eternally inclined toward loyalty to "humanity" rather than to America, to the "abstraction" of peace at whatever the going price. They advocated sharing atomic secrets with the enemy in order to nullify the weapon.

I regarded these collective attitudes as idiotic, but I was slow to condemn them as subversive, and I would be of that mind all the way. In Baltimore I was visited by an army colonel attached to the CIA. He asked me to report anything suspicious about a Hopkins physicist with a strong accent who had recently become my neighbor. I demurred at turning sleuth. He reminded me that my reserve commission was that of a major, and that I was hearing orders from a colonel. I knew that foreigners were stealing our scientific secrets. Never lose a war!

"Yes, sir," was the necessary answer, but I did nothing more and allowed my reserve commission to lapse.

10.

The Truman Hammer

IN THE WHITE HOUSE RECEIVING LINE for a press corps party, President Truman gave me a facetious wink with his warm handshake. I deduced later that the rougish greeting happened because one of his Secret Service men was once a McDonogh School student of mine (the first person I knew inside the Mansion), that the youngster had tipped the President about the stranger in his house.

I had several times by now crowded with the pack of reporters into the Oval Office, peered over shoulders and under elbows at the vibrant square-shouldered personality who stood, knuckles on desk, and returned crackling answers to Merriman Smith and May Craig (always "Smitty" and "Miss May") and a few others up close. I was seen and heard, but had never before met a president.

Recognition by the mighty, be it ever so slight, tickles the vanity; I was prepared to like Mr. Truman from the first, and it was a majority position in the postwar capital. I was a registered Democrat who voted Liberty League, and soon was emotionally attached to the 80th Congress which functioned under the so-called Coalition—a union of Republicans and Southern Democrats.

Except for hurling frequent and regular vetoes at Capitol Hill, the new President's immediate concern was foreign affairs—chiefly what turned out to be the protracted conflict with Soviet Russia, and a costly protectorate over the Jewish homeland of Israel.

Until my acquaintance widened around town, I relied heavily

61

on reading. This included a *Foreign Affairs* article which had appeared in August '47 and been made required reading by my then-employer Willard Kiplinger. He was far-seeing, and the piece, "The Sources of Soviet Conduct" by "Mr. X," would still be in the news when I was writing during the early administration of Ronald Reagan. The pseudonym was that of George F. Kennan, first director of the State Department's Policy Planning Staff, and his message was for "containment." The Russian expansion already had reached mid-Europe, the Kurile Islands and North Korea in Asia and the borders of Iran, Turkey and Greece in the Eastern Mediterranean.

No doubt Kennan spoke for the Truman Administration, but he spoke with a teasing ambiguity that combined the Delphi Oracle and *Macbeth*'s witches. At times the Policy Planner seemed to mean military restraint; at other times, political palaver. In his closing statement, Kennan sounded one of those uncertain U.S.A. trumpet calls.

"The thoughtful observer of Russian-American relations will find no cause for complaint in the Kremlin's challenge to American society. He will rather experience a certain gratitude for a Providence which, by providing the American people with an implacable challenge, has made their security as a nation dependent on their pulling themselves together and accepting the responsibilities of moral and political leadership that history plainly intended them to bear."

What did he mean—that Russian communism was a disguised blessing for us? Should we come out fighting? Or come out jawboning? Or both? Many years later Kennan with others would propose a pledge of "No first use," which meant, if implemented, no use at all by the U.S.A. of the atomic weapon. This, I would write in the 1980s, was "Judas-goat" leadership. To me Kennan's Mr. X implied an ambiguous conclusion as well as a coy authorship, but previously there had been a positive statement.

In the *Atlantic* of November '45, Dr. Albert Einstein wrote that "war is inevitable" while sovereign nations exist. He proposed that they, not the Bomb, should be abolished. "Do I fear world government?" he asked. "Of course I do. But I fear still more . . . war of wars."

Dr. Einstein's assumption was that World Government would be the only government never to have a civil war or rebellion. History simply would not endorse this notion since every country from time's beginning suffered insurrections. Therefore, I concluded, the Bomb would always be with us, always in some arsenal or another, and this much must be acknowledged.

Further, rather than merge the United States with Marxism, theocracy, militarism, cannibalism and anarchy around the globe, I reasoned that we go it alone. We should use the Bomb to re-insure American independence. The more I contemplated atomic monopoly, then enjoyed by us, the more I rejoiced at American supremacy. In the ETO we had become accustomed to the winner's circle. Our Air Corps fighters had driven the Nazi blackguards out of the skies.

"If you see planes," a briefing officer had told the assaulters of Normandy beachheads, "don't worry—they'll be ours."

There had been solemn discussion in Truman circles about delivering the A-bomb on live targets. President Truman and Henry Stimson, his realistic Secretary of War, were affirmative.

"The final decision of where and when to drop the bombs was up to me," said Truman. "Let there be no mistake about it. I regard the bomb as a military weapon and never had any doubt that it should be used."

Secretary Stimson wrote after V-J Day, "The face of war is death. Death is the inevitable part of every order a war leader gives. The decision to use the bomb was a decision that brought death to 100,000 Japanese. But this deliberate premediated destruction̵ was our least abhorrent choice. The destruction of Hiroshima put an end to the Japanese war."

Yes, but there had been other options under discussion and some broke into print. My information came from a reporter's best source, the personal interview, this one with Rear Admiral Lewis Strauss, a Republican insider at the pre-Hiroshima debate. Strauss told me early on substantially what he later wrote in his autobiography *Men and Decisions* (1962), that he was one of several who attempted to dissuade Truman from hitting the Japanese cities.

Strauss reasoned that the harsh measure was no longer

needed by the summer of '45. Japan was frantically trying to surrender through its ambassador in Moscow. Truman and Stalin, of course, knew this and Stalin had a cynical bargain with FDR. The Russians notified Japan that their Neutrality Pact would not be renewed after April 5, 1945. The Japanese assumed that the terms gave them a full year's cancellation notice. Foreign Minister Koki Hirota thought he had this period of grace with a chance to extend the treaty. Russia declared war on Japan on August 8, '45.

"My proposal," Strauss told me, "was that we demonstrate the uranium bomb on Japan's great redwood forest. I thought it a pity to destroy such a treasure of natural beauty, but preferable to incinerating all those people."

Strauss was one of several soldiers and civilians—Eisenhower and Spaatz, Arthur Compton and Edward Teller, among them— who felt that surrender could be brought about by A-bombing inanimate objects. Uninhabited islands in the open sea were proposed. Teller wanted to light up the Japanese sky with a high altitude explosion. But President Truman had geopolitical advice. He seemed converted to the argument known as "the Russian factor." He was speaking of Russians and not Japanese when he said of the bomb just before meeting with Stalin at Potsdam: "If it explodes—and I think it will—I will certainly have a hammer on those boys."

Gradualism was the pace in these portentous discussions. The initial influence on the new President was a legacy from FDR, the holdover "assistant president" (official title: Director of War Mobilization) James F. Byrnes. He had accompanied Roosevelt to the Yalta conference with Stalin and Churchill. Byrnes knew all and Truman virtually nothing about the personal relationships of the Big Three, their plans for spheres of influence in the postwar world, least of all about the atomic fission superbomb still untested in New Mexico.

President Truman gratefully, on July 3, '45, appointed Byrnes his secretary of state, realistically his "assistant president for foreign affairs." The President took Byrnes to Potsdam to meet with the top policymakers of Russia and Britain between VE and VJ Days. Byrnes, expecting to be Roosevelt's 1944 running mate,

still smarting from the disappointment, was somewhat patronizing toward Truman to whom he began to write "Dear Harry"
instead of Mr. President. It was Byrnes who taught Truman to
think of "atomic diplomacy" in dealing with Soviet Russia.

"Simply put, the bomb was a new found power," writes Prof.
Robert L. Messer in his nicely documented *The End Of An Alliance* (1982) based on Byrnes and Truman papers. "To politicians such as Truman and Byrnes, power is to be used. . . . .
[They] did not consider it malevolent. . . . Stimson, too, told
Truman that the new weapon promised to be America's 'master
card' in the diplomatic game with the Soviet Union. In a stroke,
the United States had drawn this winning card in that contest."

Truman hoped that the A-bomb would let him dominate nego-
tiations with the Russians. Blackmail was not considered. Byrnes
spoke of "the gun behind the door." The expression, stick-and-
carrot, ran through their conversations. But Truman's diary for
May 22, '45 is explicit:

". . . I knew what I wanted and that I intended to get it—peace
for the world for at least 90 years. That Poland, Rumania, Bul-
garia, Cxeckosovakia [sic], Austria, Yugo-Slavia [sic], Latvia,
Lithuania, Estonia et. al. made no difference to U.S. interests
only so far as World Peace is concerned."

East Europe was impressed in Truman's mind because between the summits of Yalta and Potsdam, Russia had begun to
stake out its advancing empire. But more immediate was the
ongoing war of the Far East. If the A-bomb was loosed on human
targets, Truman knew he could call the tune in Nippon. Instead
of dividing the rule there, as in Germany, an American procon-
sul would be the postwar solution. Non-lethal plans might work
but the only sure way to assert American authority was chosen by
Truman—the frightful demonstration of the devastating
weapon, and a will to use it on human targets.

Despite President Truman's breezy way down through the
years of disclosing and defending his historic decision, it could
not have come easily. Many of the scientific advisors, notably the
unsentimental thinker, Edward Teller, considered the atomic
device more than artillery—it was to him a supernatural phenomenon. My own belief on some incomplete but persuasive

evidence is that Truman saw more than one dimension of the Russian factor.

He could not rely on Stalin's promises, but there was a way to enforce them. Instead of bombing a Japanese forest or the open sea, why not the Siberian tundra? If it came to that, instead of Japanese cities, why not Russian military installations? Why not Moscow?

This was not quite rank speculation on my part—yet it was nothing I could write as hard fact. It was enough, however, to cause me to take sides in my columns against the nuclear-bred psychosis and craven peace-mongering of the intellectualists who seemingly ran the liberal press. Milovan Djilas, the anti-Tito communist, would say it well in a 1979 interview, ". . . the West has inflicted certain psychological wounds on itself which have no parallel in the Soviet Union . . . the antinuclear propaganda . . . constant harping on mega-deaths . . . cui bono? The answer is obvious."

The Soviet Union from 1945 on benefited. While the United States was being fear-fed, the Russian people heard nothing of nuclear horrors and were being prepared in due time to survive and win the "unwinnable" war. When I wrote to that effect, I would sometimes get encouragement from Admiral Hyman Rickover or General Albert Wedemeyer, or an opportunity to talk to Dr. Teller or Rep. Craig Hosmer, a believer in nuclear power. But it was nearly 20 years after my talk with Lewis Strauss that I found even semi-hard information that President Truman had literally earthshaking plans for his "hammer."

In 1974 two journalists were researching a biography of Dr. Teller. They were Stanley Blumberg, a science writer, and Gwinn Owens, of Westinghouse Broadcasting Group and later of the Baltimore *Sun-Papers.* Teller told them he was "convinced that the tragic surprise bombing [of Japan] was not necessary." If not necessary, why was it done? To get an answer, Blumberg-Owens went to Richard G. Hewlett, historian of the Atomic Energy Commission. At Hewlett's office in Germantown, Maryland, the authors posed this bare-boned proposition: ". . . that Japan was A-bombed not to win the war, which was already won, but to impress the Russians and to make them more tractable after the war."

Hewett responded, according to the Blumberg-Owens book on Teller, *Energy* and *Conflict*:

> "I have had some interesting exchanges with people who were involved with Stimson in the War Department. I submitted some evidence which I thought, at the time, indicated that at least they were thinking about the Russian equation. The initial reaction was 'Oh, no, we never thought about that at all, that was never in our minds.' And then when I presented this piece of paper that had a somewhat ambiguous statement in it, the man said, 'By golly, I think you have something there. It is obvious that I wrote that; I must have written it. I don't remember anything about it—it really shocks me to see it. But I guess you're right. We must have been thinking about that to some extent.'"

The question remains: Which is more believable—that the bomb was dropped on a beaten and surrendering enemy, or dropped to impress, to warn, to influence a powerful rival for control of the world? I found the second theory more credible. Truman's poised hammer kept the Russians from demanding a joint occupation of Japan in 1945 and later. So long as we had the monopoly, or held the superiority, we were able to force relative moderation on Russian expansionism. There would be plenty of bomb rattling among presidents ahead. Truman did so to bolster MacArthur at a critical time in Korea. His Secretary of Defense, Louis Johnson, floated a trial balloon to test the climate for a strike at the Russian mainland. John Foster Dulles coined phrases like "agonizing reappraisal" and "massive retaliation." President Eisenhower, in his book, *Waging Peace,* tells how he sent nuclear threats to Peking through neutral chancelleries. President Kennedy faced down Khrushchev in the Cuban missile crisis of '62 when our strategic advantage was preponderant.

The oneness in all this is that we had a unspecified policy for nuclear strike under leadership of both parties. Yet we did not implement the policy when it was viable. There were reasons why not. Public opinion at home had been saturated with guilt. Political opinion among our allies was one very close to panic. At the shadowy point where the USSR achieved nuclear parity, the hammer lost weight as a persuader and pulverizer. It's plain that we lost our nerve before we lost our clout.

That unclocked moment of nuclear equilibrium had not been reached in the autumn of 1950 when I went by engagement to a Pentagon interview with Louis Johnson, Secretary of Defense. I had access here because Secretary Johnson had been a Clarksburg lawyer in my boyhood and was often in our West Virginia and Maryland homes.

President Truman in late summer became the first human being to act as *de facto* Commander of a world government, the U.N. He invoked a war-making clause of the U.N. charter and ordered U.S. ground forces into battle. He was counting on U.N. member nations to join him in stopping the Red Korean invasion of the South. It was a multiple event. Russia had armed the Northern communists with high-grade conventional weapons. The President, over Senator Taft's vehement protests, had joined an undeclared war on an Asian peninsula where we had no visible national interests. It was a fight between Moscow's client state and one of our own, the miscalled Republic of Korea. It was the first reply to George Kennan's containment quiz. We were going to resist communist expansion by force, where negotiation was absent. But would we fight to win?

I opened my Louis Johnson interview cautiously. An abrupt lunge often brings a slammed door. The Secretary needed no probing. He knew there was but one subject between us. He pointed to his desk saying, "You see that white telephone?" He addressed me with emphasis.

"Yes, I do."

"Well, I'm waiting for it to ring. It's a direct line to the White House."

"Yes, I know."

"We've got no business fighting a ground war in Korea nor anywhere. The President wanted his budget cut, so we agreed to ask for only $15 billion. That meant practically to disband the Army."

"Yes, sir."

"Now I ask you—why keep a Navy? Who the hell is there to fight?"

I knew that, along with Chairman Tydings of the Senate Armed Services, Johnson had obliged the White House by effectively beaching the Navy. He went on.

"So do we slug it out in Korea? No, we don't. We've got to go where the trouble is."

I was going to make him say it. "Where do you mean, Mr. Secretary? Do you mean Moscow?"

"Yes, I mean Moscow."

There were only the two of us. If he didn't suddenly go off-record, I had the big story. But he put no strings to the interview. He had been a colonel in World War I. He had been head of the American Legion. He had raised the funds that moved the Truman campaign train to victory over Dewey. He was big, burly in person and personality. Critics said that in "cutting the fat," Johnson had cut the "muscle" of the Defense Department. He had antagonized the Secretary of State and the Joint Chiefs of Staff. But he sounded more right than wrong to me. He wanted to win.

"I mean Moscow," Johnson repeated. "It's where the heart of the trouble is. Well, we've got a fleet of B-29s and we've got the U-235 bomb. Why bleed to death in Korea?"

I wrote my story with due regard for its rough edges. Louis Johnson was a political appointee, not popular anywhere in town. He had given this sensational story to an individual reporter, instead of calling a press conference where he couldn't claim to be misquoted. I suspected that President Truman had egged him on to experiment with a touchy subject just as respectable Republicans egged on Joe McCarthy. President Truman yearned to swing the atomic hammer. He proved this on November 30, 1950, by artfully hinting at a White House press conference, which I attended, that the A-bomb was available for use against the Chinese and that the decision rested with the field commander, General MacArthur.

Reporters stampeded for telephones, Prime Minister Atlee winged across the Atlantic. White House press officers issued "clarifying statements." I no longer doubted that Harry Truman carried the fastest gun in the Western world. Timid advisors kept it clamped in his holster. But Truman set the nuclear policy for follow-on presidents who had the urge but not the will. Time ticked on. Our nuclear arsenal sank from supremacy to superiority to parity to inferiority.

Louis Johnson was hounded from office and is not remembered as a major figure. But he was my friend, and he was Harry Truman's friend until cut down by political alley fighters. Louis Johnson understood the unwritten Truman Doctrine—the preventive war that would have made all the difference in the national decline that lay before us. I became sure of this when Johnson, out of office, wrote me to say that I had accurately reported and interpreted our Pentagon interview.

11.

The Wildfire Spread
of Internationalism

CARLYLE: "The history of the world is but the biography of great men."

VOLTAIRE: "History is little less than a picture of human crimes and misfortunes."

WASHINGTON: "It is our true policy to steer clear of permanent alliances with any portion of the foreign world. . . . There can be no greater error than to expect or calculate upon real favors from nation to nation."

MONROE: "The American continents . . . are henceforth not to be subjects for future colonization by any European powers."

J.Q. ADAMS: "America does not go abroad in search of monsters to destroy."

BRYAN: "Behold a Republic gradually but surely becoming the supreme moral factor in disputes."

TOCQUEVILLE: "The Anglo-American relies on personal interest to accomplish his ends and gives free scope to the unguided strength and common sense of the people; the Russian centers all the authority of society in a single arm. The principal instrument of the former is freedom; of the latter, servitude."

ACHESON: "This country must not stand by while
the little principality of Moscovy ex-
pands across the world."

With another and non-competitive reporter I was interviewing
Secretary of State Acheson in his Foggy Bottom office and received this statement. Years later on the day Acheson's 1970
Pulitzer Prize for History was announced, I chanced to sit with
him at the Metropolitan Club senior luncheon table where, with
pardonable pride, he'd made a rare appearance to accept con-
gratulations. *Present At The Creation* was a deserved winner, given
some omissions which a subsequent biographer, David S.
McLellan, in 1976 supplied in the best of taste.

To me that one memorable and simplistic quote from the
Secretary would always set the limits to my admiration of a
notably splendid man. In the huffy resentment of Moscovy's
outreach, surely the most salient characteristic of every energetic
state in history, Acheson revealed two of his persistent faults as a
statesman.

He was always patronizing what he regarded as lesser breeds,
the working press and the general public. Also, he repeatedly
showed an unfirm grasp of history and statesmanship. I felt this
long before it was ruefully documented in the McLellan admiring biography. As Under Secretary, Acheson thought Churchill's
famous Iron Curtain speech at Fulton, Missouri, a diplomatic
disaster and pointedly did not attend a New York reception in
Churchill's honor. Subsequently, Secretary Acheson's attitude toward Asian communism, in McLellan's sorrowful phrase, "be-
trays an understandable, albeit regrettable tendency to
underestimate the Red Chinese, which was to have tragic consequences at the time of the Korean War." Acheson's complacency
toward communist dangers on both Western and Eastern fronts
would be largely unremarked factors in his on-coming encounters with Joe McCarthy.

Acheson may well have been the best of the post-Roosevelt
Secretaries of State, but this is not to grant him an historical
superlative. He was not consumed with jealousy like Byrnes, not
a graven image like Marshall, not flatulent with ego-evangelism

like Dulles, not feckless like Rusk. Handsome, stylish, well-spoken, patrician and idealistic, Acheson marred a selfless and patriotic record by quixotic and butter-fingered relations with the press and public. I was "present at the creation" of several blunders and wrote about them.

In the State Department auditorium I heard him theatrically quote the Sermon on the Mount when vowing "never to turn my back on Alger Hiss," his friend and convicted perjurer in the notorious communist espionage case. Like many others at Acheson's most memorable press conference, I admired the moral courage of the Secretary's grandstand play. He had a hard choice between personal loyalty and public duty, and I was not among the first to condemn him. Acheson had his own doubts, for he immediately offered his resignation to the doughty President who refused to listen.

But as a regular attendant of Acheson's appearances at Senate hearings, my esteem weakened and crumbled. At the Foreign Relations sessions, he told the Senators that his "friendship" was not "lightly given," and that he held Donald Hiss, a law partner, very dear, while he knew Alger only casually. Many years later and after his death, the Secretary appeared as a minor character in historian Allen Weinstein's *Perjury: The Hiss-Chambers Case* (1978) where it turned out that Acheson knew Alger quite well. "I had the benefit of Dean Acheson's advice last night," wrote Hiss to John Foster Dulles, August 6, 1948. On the previous day, Alger and Donald with their lawyers had held a strategy discussion in Acheson's law office just prior to Alger's testimony on Capitol Hill where he committed the perjury that sent him to prison. Had any member of the Congress or press corps known and revealed this and other subsequently discovered facts, there would have been little left of Acheson's assumed nobility. One reporter, Robert J. Donovan, in his 1982 biography of Harry Truman, summed up by hindsight: "If the members of the Senate had known that Acheson had advised Hiss on the latter's congressional testimony, they might have rejected Acheson's nomination. . . . Even if Acheson had survived the Senate vote, the knowledge . . . would have been another calamity for President Truman."

Donovan's was a cautious understatement; it's my belief that both high-toned officials would have been convicted of perjury. As it happened, Acheson was wept over, honored and sung at his death in 1971.

My own feelings toward Acheson changed from dislike to distrust during the Truman incumbancy. I heard the Secretary assure Senator Taft in committee that the peacetime occupation of Western Europe under the Atlantic Alliance was a temporary expediency, which the Secretary had every reason to disbelieve. A dialogue with Senator Hickenlooper was adamantly specific:

Hickenlooper: "[Are we] going to be expected to send substantial troops over there as a more or less permanent contribution to the development of these countries' capacity to resist?"

Acheson: "The answer to that question, Senator, is a clear and absolute 'No.'"

I heard the National Press Club speech in which Acheson excluded Korea from the U.S. defense perimeter. It would be difficult to find another single statement by a high national official of any country which inadvertently triggered a lengthy war and set up an indefinite armed truce. To his discredit, Acheson denied the blunder by evasion in his autobiographical writings. Whatever his rationalization, Acheson was the point man for the 40-year presence of U.S. divisions and their "dependents" in Western Europe and at the DMZ between South and North Korea. His name will have to stand to the record of these American hostages.

Groton, Yale, Harvard Law School, wealthy by marriage and achievement, high-born and well-read, Acheson failed in my observation to comprehend the grand outlines and relentless tides of history. Wiser men than he—a few quoted at the head of this chapter—could have taught him the larger views. There have always been world trends in the dynamics of peoples who move their armies far from home base. More stable nations have planned self-defense that does not include shelter behind fragile alliances and reliance on treaties written in quibbling legalities— mere scraps of paper.

Nothing was gained by Acheson when he repeatedly talked down to reporters and bandied double-entendres with Senators.

The large reality of his day was that the American republic-into-democracy had long ago become as expansive as the upstart Moscovy principality; scores of small but restless peoples had done so down the centuries. America and Russia had long been on a collision course. Manifest destiny in both instances had more to do with reality than with right and wrong. Old Hickory, democracy's first "border captain," slaughtered and resettled the hapless Indian tribes, much as the Czars did the Mongols, Chinese and almost countless ethnic groups in the path of empire.

Both superpowers were driving toward the Pacific from opposite directions. Long before Lenin and Stalin followed the Romanoff tradition of Eurasian land-grabbing, American imperialists had marched across the continent and taken ship for further conquests. Early Americans—Washington, Monroe, the Adamses and their helpers—had counseled for local, then continental, then hemispheric defense, but the advice went unheeded when Jackson, Wilson and the Roosevelts could not be contained by the forefathers' principles. The Russian nation drove ahead without the hindrance of such advice as the Farewell Address.

Was the conflict irrepressible? In any case, there is no way to understand Tocqueville and the Cold War without objectively considering the record of both antagonists. Acheson was not first or alone in leveling the finger of guilt at the opponents, nor in striking the pose of American injured innocence. While I was unalterably for "never lose a war" and entirely my-country-right-or-wrong in any on-going contest, I believed our leaders should come clean. They should acknowledge to the people that our sincerest good-will foreign policies had a way of degenerating into bought friendship, subsidized dictators, foreign mercenaries to fight freedom fighters, and assassins to remove troublesome leaders. Reporters would dig out the facts that government concealed. What started as genuine foreign aid and democratic reconstruction became Cold War imperialism and was everywhere resented and repudiated by the recipient peoples. It was all deplorable. But had we passed the point of no return? Had we no choice between a death-struggle and progressive surrender? No American leader dared an audacious answer until President Reagan opted for a crash program of rearmament.

Russia had set its European frontier in mid-Germany. I remember standing in awe at the solemn beauty of the Soviet War
Memorial in Treptower Park, East Berlin, 1959. This military
cemetery of the USSR holds five thousand officers and men who
died taking Berlin. The architectural landscaping is unsur-
passed. In the front court of a sweeping oval is the statue of a
woman who sits and weeps, symbolic of the motherland mourn-
ing her dead. Lowered flags of red granite for the sixteen Soviet
republics stand in rank. At a hilltop looms the bronze likeness of
a Soviet soldier. His right hand holds a sword over a broken
swastika. His arm supports a rescued German child.

The whole is breath-taking to see. I did not at first grasp the
full meaning, until the lady at my side, my wife, murmured, "It
is their boundary stake. They will never retreat from this place."

Simultaneously, NATO had advanced to the Brandenburg
Gate between the two Berlins. I would several times visit Supreme Allied Headquarters in France and Belgium and find it
significant that the Supreme Commander was never European,
always American, as if the Allies might well sit out the next
death-dance.

The U.S.A. and the USSR stood nose to nose when Mr. Truman took office and asked White House correspondents to "pray
for me." At that time, or soon afterwards, he knew that he had
the means, in the atomic bomb monopoly, to slash the Gordian
Knot before it tightened. Not just the warhawks of the day were
beginning to think in that direction. As level-headed a patriot as
Henry Cabot Lodge asked Acheson in an executive session of
Foreign Relations whether a preventive war against the Soviets
would not be justified. Acheson replied that such talk, let alone
such action, "brings on us all the troubles we seek to avoid." The
Secretary added that Russia's scientific ability to break the U.S.
monopoly "is a matter about which I think there is very much
doubt." The new President for some time had full confidence,
and no doubt, about America's ability to maintain atomic supremacy through its engineering skills.

President Truman would always incline to do his "damndest"
for his country's good. At the time of taking office he had not hit
his stride, nor brought Acheson to the Cabinet, but moved with

an uneven gradualism that would take him to the threshhold of atomic employment. But his first major address at the U.N. charter convention, San Francisco, June 28, 1945, was not the Truman that we came to know. He said, "Let us not fail to grasp this supreme chance to establish worldwide rule of reason—to create an enduring peace under the guidance of God."

President Truman had not yet learned that his keywords—"peace and God"—were inappropriate for dealing with the USSR. They were not even his own words, observed Cabell Phillips of the *New York Times*. "The voice was the voice of Harry Truman, but the words were the words of Franklin Roosevelt distilled through the facile pen of Sam Rosenman." Soon the man from Independence, Missouri, found himself. One of his least remembered acts after the German surrender was to halt Lend Lease cargoes to Russia. Ships at sea were told to turn back; those loading in port were told to stop it.

Unfortunately, the Roosevelt momentum was still running strong in American public opinion, and Truman had to modify these cancellation orders. Still, an entirely new attitude toward the Red dictatorship had been indicated.

Going into the second half of the 20th century, the U.S.A. had roughly a half-hundred entangling alliances. Another snarl was the popular fallacy about interdependence on the rest of the world. It became a common misconception that something behooved us to repeal our economic liberty and to share know-how and raw materials with all mankind. History was there to teach us something different. Only chocolate and coffee are unavailable products, it has been deduced. Dependence on imports in so vast a nation as ours is laziness and greed. Self-sufficiency is possible through our proven ingenuity with synthetics, provided we are willing to adapt an austere lifestyle. When Indonesian rubber was cut off by the Japanese, we turned to the synthetic product. There is no deep necessity for chrome-clad gas-guzzling vehicles and color television for every American household. Yet we have had no post-World War II president, or any major statesman, to speak these self-evident truths.

It is well to remember, however, that we did have 20th-century presidents who could be reasonably satisfied with the blessings of freedom and the work ethic. The one exception, Theodore Roosevelt, blustered much, but save in the instance of Panama lived up to his Inaugural promise. "While ever careful to refrain from wrongdoing others, we must be no less insistent that we are not wronged ourselves." More well-adjusted men—Taft and Eisenhower, Coolidge and Hoover—kept vigil and that was all. The despised Harding (he drank less than Grant and LBJ; his sex life was tame beside Jack Kennedy's and Nelson Rockefeller's) presided over a four-power naval disarmament that failed because foreigners cheated. In a forgotten action, Harding renewed the spirit of the undefended Canadian-American border. He never got his due from the supranational opinion-makers.

I came to conclude that no American president should ignore J.Q. Adams's resolve against "going about in search of monsters to destroy." Henry Adams definitely believed that McKinley had a screw loose ("an uncommonly dangerous politician"). Thomas Woodrow Wilson had ended his Princeton University tenure before my day there, but his spirit lingered. My English department adviser and close friend, Professor Frank McDonald, admired the fluency and precision of language with which the University president conducted faculty meetings. But Walter Karp in *The Politics of War* epitomized Wilson's ruling passion: "Vainglory."

Vanity, a thirst for glorification, predominated in our worst presidents—McKinley to Nixon. My column "Fence Post in a Hurricane" featured the conversion of Senator Arthur Vandenberg from isolation to internationalism. It was no "straw in the wind" as it was being interpreted in some places. I did not verify the details until 1980 when I read Ronald Steel's book on Walter Lippmann; but I had already happened upon clues of my own as to Vandenberg's switch. It was not brought about so much by intellectual conviction as by political ambition and romantic stirrings of the aging male.

Steel's biography relates that Lippmann and James Reston convinced Big Van that isolation was "old hat" for presidential aspirations. These two correspondents wrote the Senator's Damascus Road speech where he proclaimed his conversion to a political religion that was not his own. The January 1945 address sent Vandenberg in search of the 1948 GOP presidential nomination in the season when Truman was considered a goner. But I had already learned that the Lippmann-Reston ghostwriting was not the entire reason for Van's aspiration to larger greatness. There was a Mata Hari angle to the story.

No Senator of his day was more recognizable than Arthur Vandenberg. He cruised the upper chamber like a stately galleon beneath the press gallery. His reputation among reporters ranged from portentous to pompous. I knew the Michigan Senator only at a distance and in a crowd. Upon becoming a full-time columnist I systematically rounded the four floors of the Senate Office Building (the only SOB of that time) and through patience managed a meeting with 95 of the 96 Senators. I had called at Vandenberg's office, talked to Van Junior, his chief assistant, but never got to meet the father.

Therefore, as a commuter to Baltimore, I was lucky enough to spot Senator Vandenberg one day in Union Station through which I passed daily and where I sometimes took a high-ball at the Savarin restaurant. Here was the chance to introduce myself, but I saw the Senator was not alone. I thought little of it the first time. Then, at other times I saw Big Van with a lady who unmistakably was not a wife, daughter or secretary. Even at a plebian Savarin barroom table Mitzi Sims had the uptown look of Embassy Row. Adjectives used by society writers for her included "smart, dashing, stunning."

Why the rendezvous at such a well-traveled place? Well, it was convenient to Capitol Hill. It fitted Edgar Allan Poe's theory that the best place to "plant the knife" is the most conspicuous spot, where it would be overlooked. I never attempted a scandal story. But knowledge is power. In journalism the reporter can never know too much. I took my information to the SOB and to the vehement isolationist, Senator George Malone, Republican of Nevada. It turned out that Van's liaison and the trysting place had become GOP gossip. The Old Guard had little good will for the switch-hitting Michigander. The lady involved was an unregistered lobbyist married to a British diplomat. It was a time when Whitehall grappled without scruple for the Marshall Plan, the British Loan and NATO.

"A man oughtn't to learn foreign policy with his pecker," Malone roared to me in his office.

In times ahead, a loyal Michigan reporter assured me that the Senator, while "truly enamoured" had only "affection" for Mitzi Sims. Van Junior, I learned, was not fond of Hazel, his step-mother. He approved of Mitzi and his father's autumnal romance. Hazel was complaisant about it.

If Vandenberg thought that going bipartisan would improve his presidential chances, he miscalculated. When he deserted the diehards of the right wing, they deserted him. "Do you want me to be President?" the Senator asked a close friend of the press, who repeated the conversation to me. "I don't think I could live out four years of the pressure." But he was under the mistletoe, and willing for the nomination kiss. And at the '48 Republican Convention in Philadelphia, one morning we reporters found that a smear sheet on Van had been distributed to our seats overnight. I recollect only one columnist, John O'Donnell of the *New York Daily News,* who wrote the story. Whatever its effect, if any, Vandenberg ceased to be a prominent candidate.

Political internationalism proved ego-inflationary in most postwar candidates for the White House. Taft had no vainglory, Dewey had some, Vandenberg and Stassen had it like a raging fever. Harold Stassen, the "boy governor," became a career-long victim of it.

I first met the strapping, blond, poker-faced Stassen in 1947 when he turned up in Washington. He was the first to line up for president, and the last to have any chance. His only qualification was that he had an assignment from the Navy to attend the UN Charter session. He used this to make himself a national figure.

Stassen may not have calculated the mischievous bent of the Washington press corps. He rented an office suite on Connecti-cut Avenue across from the Mayflower Hotel. "Governor, who's paying the rent?" He had a private airplane which whisked him to the pressure points. "Governor, whose plane is it, anyhow?" I'd asked that question, and he quipped, "Would you like a ride?" Tom Stokes, a friendly fellow-columnist, joined me in finding a partial list of Stassen bankrollers. There were no sinis-ter agents on it, only a group of midwest millers and lumber merchants. Evidently, they had pooled money and taken shares in this candidate as they might have in a racehorse or prize fighter. If by some fluke he won, the backers became investors in Stassen's project, a World State.

A World State . . . I soon began to travel it, and was abroad once or twice a year for the next three decades. Except for Red China, I touched down nearly everywhere. I hope I was objective. Neutral I could not be. I opposed nearly every feature of our foreign policy. I found pretty much what I expected to find.

Germany in the late '40s. Former war buddies had stayed on in the occupation forces, and I looked them up. The ex-flyboys and their families never had it so good. Housed sometimes in palatial hotels, sometimes in picturesque dwellings of a fast-recovering Reich, the onetime bombardiers and aerial gunners shopped with bargain prices at the PX and on the black market. Their wives could afford unaccustomed finery in expensive dresses and rare antiques. American servicemen lived as benign conquerors are entitled to live. More than once, while we drank and reminisced, I would be importuned, "Now, Alecks, don't go home and write anything to spoil our racket."

But it was all too easy to foresee the "Yankee go home" era which wasn't far ahead. Idle troops and jealous natives made us much unloved. Neither group was any safer from the Soviet buildup.

Eastern Europe in the mid '50s. I rode the Hungarian airlift in '56, interviewed refugees crossing at Salzburg, stopped in Munich and the Allied Supreme Headquarters near Paris. Some Hungarians contended that they were incited to rebellion by Radio Free Europe, then got no help from our troops. Most Germans and Frenchmen expressed horror that a U.S. intervention would trigger another war. In the NATO headquarters, ex-Nazi officers were fraternizing with the victors.

Who had won that war, anyhow? Everybody knew that the winners were massing beyond the Elbe River. During that '56 election year I brought my wife over to London to visit friends. Later that same year we went to British Nassau on one of my stories. The English on both these islands were as cold toward us as well-bred people can be. "Why hasn't Eisenhower helped us recapture Suez?" they would ask.

Middle East in the late '50s. In a military administration office at Cairo, I asked the officer about his need for the requested medium range fighter-bombers. For defense they were the wrong weapons. For assault they could only be intended for use against Israel. The Egyptian yelled at me that U.S. support for Israel kept the war going. He howled abuse at America's stupidity—I walked out on him.

At Israel's Red Sea port of Eilat, I could look into three countries, all at war, while sea traffic flowed peacefully between them. Flying back to Tel Aviv, I arched my eyebrows to learn that at the scattered military camps communications were operated by girls who cohabitated with the soldiers. My escort officer rejected any notion of hankypanky while on duty. Arabs and Jews made war, not love.

Berlin in the early '60s. Vice President Johnson told me after the Bay of Pigs, "It wouldn't have happened if I'd been president." I flew with him on Air Force 2 to face the Berlin Wall—only rolls of barbed wire at this time. While LBJ pressed the flesh in throngs of West Berliners, Gen. Lucius Clay (wartime governor of the city) told me that he was going in civilian clothes through the Brandenburg Gate into East Berlin. I met him on his return and he said, "If the Vice President would go through the Gate, I think the East Berliners would tear down the Wall with bare hands. But there are four Soviet divisions on the Polish border, and I'd make no further predictions."

Far East in the early '60s. In South Korea, an armed ceasefire had existed for a decade in what was still called a UN police action. I searched for the foreign peacekeepers who supposedly shared the job with Americans. I found only a British sergeant-major doing paperwork. Looking across the DMZ, I realized that the U.S.A. had the Red tiger by the tail.

Southern Africa in the mid-'60s. Visiting South Africa as a guest of its government, I resolved to stay off racial matters. The humiliating practice of apartheid was all about; so was the slow and unsatisfactory reform by the dominant whites. I visited the faculty of a black college, a gold mine, a prison, the home of a noted sculptor and interviewed political, military and financial leaders. There was no mistaking that this nation of wealth and culture had real value to the Western World. When I asked one of its top officials what was South Africa's most bothersome problem, he did not name the racial one.

"You know who," he answered phonetically.

It took me a moment to translate, "UNO—the United Nations Organization."

What South Africa most desired was to be left alone.

Moving northward into Rhodesia, I saw a 19th-century British colony in the process of becoming a Black republic. Still further north, I found the Congo River dividing a peaceful (but not for long) French colony from a Belgian colony in open rebellion. A U.S. attache took me to luncheon and discounted the native rebels.

"They're not well armed and not very brave," he said, but soon there would be Soviet weapons and Soviet-trained leadership.

Far East in the mid-'60s. In the Hotel Caravelle, I knelt and prayed—just in case. I had volunteered for two combat missions. American "advisors" at this point made up the aircrews and sometimes a Vietnamese soldier rode deadhead as a token. The arrangement was changing as the Viets were given U.S. aircraft and instructions. Interviews with General Westmoreland and embassy spokesman U. Alexis Johnson encouraged my wishful thinking. With the Tall Texan now in the White House I could not believe America would lose a war.

When I expressed this view at the officers mess where the regular correspondents ate, it was greeted with derision. In a kindly attempt to educate an itinerent, "two-week wonder," a group of the war correspondents gave me a farewell dinner in a moonlit Saigon garden. They were strong in their arguments that the war was unwinnable. After dessert and brandy, we took a vote on the subject. Mine was the only optimistic opinion, and the least informed.

On five continents I found nowhere that our international foreign policy was making friends, keeping peace, winning respect. President Johnson tried to end in Vietnam what President Kennedy had begun. Nixon and Ford had to shoot their way out. Carter lost rounds to both communists and Muslims. Reagan began to restore patriotism and rev up the arms race while negotiating for arms reduction. There was no telling where we would go from here.

12.

Fall of a Titan

LONG AND PUNISHING WAS THE ROAD from Robert Taft to Ronald Reagan, a forty-year pull through Goldwater to the conservative consumation. I believed the country wanted these qualities all along and mistakenly sought them in a twice-elected Eisenhower and Nixon, who were not at all "conservative." Like all others who traveled the road, I could not see the journey's end; like all who now can look back on the march, I have the hindsight to see the shortcut.

Since the people wanted postwar conservatism, what they should have done in 1948 was to send to the presidency Robert Alfonso Taft, free enterpriser, nationalist, constitutionalist, an uncompromising, unapologetic rightwinger. He was all these things—also tactless, disorganized, opposed to consensus, impatient of fools—and thus he failed at the grand achievement of reaching the people. But the cardinal sin of vainglory was not in him. Accumulate executive power? Centralize government in Washington? Yearn to straddle the world? In Taft, all the opposite desires predominated.

Essentially a parliamentarian, not very "presidential," a believer in Congress to rule, in the "invisible hand" of capitalism to control the economy, in sea power and its extension, air power, to protect the Western Hemisphere, Senator Taft as president might have spared us much—who can say? Throughout the time that our work in Washington coincided, I had an easy come-and-go access to Taft's office. My column prospered best in his political homelands, Mid-America, the Confederate South, the Rocky Mountains, New England and California. Taft and I were

aliens in areas and colonies of the liberal eastern Establishment,
and not sorry for that. "Taft loved you," said one of his top aides
in a reminiscence session long after the Senator's death. That
expression by Lyndon Johnson, or any effusive Southerner, was
cliched and meaningless in political Washington. From Taft, if
true, it was priceless praise, and I relished it.

The running yarn of my columns tells of an interregnum—
from Taft's uncrowned reign to Reagan's ascension. Most of the
Taft story is domestic politics, little is of foreign policy, save
where the lines crossed.

"Yes, of course," said the CIA retired official whom I told of a
rescued German gunner and his drugged refrain, "Ve vin. Ve
vin." "Your gunner was well indoctrinated. Beginning in the
winter of 1941-42, Nazi generals were sending us signals. The
wehrmacht had been stopped dead at the gates of Leningrad,
Stalingrad and Moscow. The German military wanted a separate
peace, an Axis-Western alliance against Russia. Communism, the
common foe."

"But no takers on our side."

"Nope."

I think Taft would have been a taker. Fascists, he calculated at a
few million, World Communists at many million, a more fear-
some menace to the U.S.A. He believed that the fall of England,
improbable after the Battle of Britain and Hitler's invasion of
Russia, would be a lesser evil than America's plunge into World
War II. With any sort of peace, we could trade with Western
Europe. McKinley had made the Pacific a Republican ocean,
Wilson, the Atlantic a Democratic one. Taft would have given
MacArthur priority over Eisenhower, but he would have tried to
avoid the Second World War entirely instead of joining it. I asked
the CIA man why the German peace feelers, long before heavy
American bloodshed, got no attention.

"Mostly Morganthau," he answered.

Henry "The Morgue," Secretary of the Treasury, Roosevelt's
friend and neighbor, had an ignorance about finance that was a
standing press corps joke. As part of my catch up work after
leaving Kiplinger, I spent a whole afternoon buying drinks and
pumping recollections from an ex-reporter at Treasury who'd

turned airline publicist. The goofs and blunders of this cabinet officer were town gossip. How had he gotten into foreign policy? Then I remembered the Morganthau plan to turn Germany into a "cow pasture."

"Roosevelt was dying," the CIA man continued. "Morganthau pushed for this postwar policy on Germany."

After our luncheon I went back to my office and checked for references in Jim Bishop's *FDR's Last Year*. There were five citations on the scheme to make Germany into an agricultural state without heavy industry. Who would benefit more than the USSR?

Morganthau was no Red agent, but his assistant and supposed co-author of the plan was Harry Dexter White. Whittaker Chambers in 1948 fingered White as a communist spy—at which White dropped dead of a heart attack. It would be rank McCarthyism to draw conclusions without courthouse rules of evidence, but Taft was undeterred. In March 1950 he told interviewers that Joe "should keep talking and if one case doesn't work out, he should proceed to another. . . . Whether Senator McCarthy had legal evidence, whether he overstated or understated his case, is of lesser importance. The question is whether the communist influence in the State Department still exists."

Tactless? It shook up Bill White, Taft's best biographer. It horrified the Libs; Taft didn't care. If "modern" Republicans thought him beastly, he gave it no thought. He observed that the War Crime trials were lynching German and Japanese officials for offenses invented after the fact—*ex post facto*, he said, and it put the Western system of justice in cahoots with liquidation, Soviet style.

American Jewry rose up—Taft defending those Nazi oven-operators? But Taft was a proclaimed Zionist. He would use the forum of the National Conference of Christians and Jews in 1953 to denounce the United Nations, a phony peacekeeper, and to deplore America's membership. His Taft-Hartley Act would be called by Labor leaders a "slave law." But President Truman in 1946 proposed to draft striking union workers and order them back to work. Whose "slave law"? Taft took the Senate floor to denounce dictatorship and violation of the Constitution where it forbade involuntary servitude.

At first, I would quail at solo interviews in the Senator's cramped, cluttered private office. Perhaps I only thought it close quarters. He was a big man, with a large, buck-toothed face. He sat in a heavy armchair, under a blown-up photo of his whale-bodied, walrus-mustached tophatted father in the Inaugural carriage, vintage 1909. The Senator talked, like a toneless dictating machine, of budget, labor, military unification, his chairmanship of the Republican Policy Committee which effectively made him boss of the Senate—but he could be humanized by shifting the subject to the Buckeye State.

Then, he would lean toward me, lay a paw on my knee and talk about the inland commonwealth of his heart. ". . . farm families," he said, "attending the same agricultural colleges for generations, intermarrying, keeping their wealth." He went on—business firms, law firms, industrial plants, universities, union workers who gave him his majorities despite the enmity of the Labor lords.

He would snort at any mention of his alleged ignorance of the non-American world. "Why, I've traveled it all over." As a schoolboy of a wealthy family he had twice done the Grand Tour of Europe. He had gone to school in Japan; lived in the Philippines where his father was governor general; accompanied his father to the Vatican to negotiate on Catholic Church property once under Spain; was a volunteer clerk when William Howard Taft served as President and later Chief Justice.

Except for the Marshall Plan, Bob Taft voted against all the foreign entanglements. But he believed that even unnecessary wars ought to be won. He wanted MacArthur to have a free hand to unify Korea and keep the Red Chinese behind the Yalu.

He thought as flat-footedly as he walked, and I may have learned from his thinking style. Where was the logic of the gift-horse from France in New York harbor? "Give us your tired, your poor, your huddled masses . . . wretched refuse of your teeming shore." Who wanted "refuse"? I considered customs officers, immigration officials as the first line of defense against bankruptcy, unemployment, slums and crime.

Protectionism was rightly named. If conservatives feared not the hobgoblin of inconsistency, what about the Libs? Nobody could be more consistently illiberal than a Liberal. None was so blindly intolerant to opposition ideas. Senator Paul Douglas, the best of the breed, served me as an example in some forgotten matter. Afterwards, I had reason to consult Douglas; he thanked me with Quaker gentleness for the rebuke, and later wrote me.

"As I told you, one of your articles which cut me to the quick was, I think, the most constructive criticism which I have ever received. When Mrs. Douglas read it, she said, 'Paul, you should take this to heart.' In it you said I gave the impression of being excessively self-righteous and somewhat self-satisfied. After searching my heart, I decided that you might be right and really have tried since then to reduce what I think was a weakness."

In his 600-page memoir, *In the Fullness of Time*, Douglas returned to the subject.

"I was shocked to learn that critics accused me of smugness. I tried to dismiss the criticism as politically inspired but it continued, culminating in an extraordinary column by the conservative writer, Holmes Alexander. He probed my inner depths, and despite a few misconceptions, analyzed me in a way Freud would have envied. Although not unfriendly, his analysis hurt me more than any former criticism. In fact, I literally gasped with pain. . . . Although I avoided Alexander, I felt he was watching me closely. Years later I told him that, while his article had hurt me more than anything that had ever been published about me, it also helped me more. Eyeing me quizzically, he shook hands."

Afterwards, I gave Douglas my space for a guest column to express his views to my readers. I made this my habit with dissenting Libs—among them the Kennedys, Hubert Humphrey, Joe Clark, and many others. The practice broadened friendships and education. Senator John F. Kennedy got through a Labor bill which I thought helpful to businessmen, so I asked him about any favorable response from that section, and he said there was none. I wrote a column and he wrote me back, May 26, 1959:

"I want to send you a word of thanks for the very generous and skillful column you wrote ten days ago regarding the deafening silence on the Labor bill. You may be pleased to know that after your column I did receive a small accretion of correspondence regarding the Labor bill. You seem to have been more successful in achieving this result by a few pithy paragraphs than I was in many hours of debate and consultation. With best thanks and good wishes, I am

Sincerely,
Jack."

I met the striking personality, Carleton Putnam, Princeton, '24 and Columbia Law School, '32, a tall square-rigger of a Yankee. He was known for his 626-page *Theodore Roosevelt*, Vol. I., *The Formative Years* (Scribners), a critics' delight. He became an airplane pilot, board chairman of Delta Airlines, author of *High Journey* (Scribners), about his flying adventures.

Curious as to why he'd written no follow-on to the TR biography, I found he had deviated from that subject to write about immigrants. They weren't the ones of the Statue of Liberty's welcome message—they were involuntary immigrants, American Blacks. Putnam's most recent books were *Race and Reason* (1961) and *Race and Reality* (1967).

I read these. I read some commentary. Putnam's good American name had been linked by Liberal critics to Adolph Hitler's. When I solicited him for a guest column, he wrote a good one. McNaught Syndicate rejected it. His name was poison in the editorial offices.

Trouble was, Putnam had met the illiberal Liberals who tolerated no opinion but their own. He had taken scholarly issue with the Warren Court in Brown *v.* Board of Education. His books on race did not find a metropolitan publisher (they had to be subsidized) and Scribners did not encourage him to finish the Roosevelt.

Putnam's analysis of the Warren ruling on public school integration was that it would lead to racial mongrelization. He claimed it already had led to gross hypocrisy in American scholarship. Putnam wrote me:

"Even to whisper such theories in private was considered an obscenity. . . . The permissive houses that would welcome communism and pornography drew the line when it came to race. . . . I am not by nature an unkind person . . . do not hate negroes or wish them harm. . . . What I hate is the deliberate fraud regarding essential facts—with the erosion of our civilization. Regards, Carlton."

An extraordinary man, this. I saw much similarity with Charles Lindbergh—an aviator, a writer, a challenger of mass opinion, a bruised receiver of the consequences. At the time I was considering whether I should attempt this memoir, a biography of Carlton Putnam appealed to me more than doing an autobiography that covered much the same period. We had an exchange of letters and conversations. I urged him to write his story, or to help me write it. He and I had similar ideas. We both agreed that distorted scholarship, forced race mixing, runaway liberalism and intolerance were accommodative of the communist revolution. Either his story or mine would make the big points.

But Putnam demurred. He pointed out that his race books, even without a prestige publisher, had sold 100,000 copies. In them he had quoted Ortega y Gasset on "the sovereignty of the unqualified," and developed that theme. He had cited and expanded upon Lord Tweedsmuir: "The gutters have exuded a poison that bids fair to infect the world. The beggar on horseback rides more roughshod over the helpless than the cavalier." He had exposed the cropped quotation on the Jefferson Memorial where the second half is omitted beyond the semicolon. Jefferson had written:

"Nothing is more certainly written in the book of fate than that these two people are to be free; nor is it less certain that the two races, equally free, cannot live under the same government."

Later on, Edmund Morris in notes on his splendid *The Rise of Theodore Roosevelt* (1979) said of Putnam's unfinished TR biography (the two writers had never met): "It is a tragedy of American biography that this gravely neglected masterpiece was never followed by other volumes."

I wanted Putnam's *High Journey*, a book about physical adventure, to be extended into the areas of philosophy, social protest, and interpretive history of our times. He decided to stand on his record.

I returned to write this book. I saw the Taft era as prologue to Reagan's. In the interim, our ship of state was on the rocks. Liberal anti-protectionism had resulted in loss of our industrial primacy to Japan. Liberal immigration policies (or non-policies) found us swamped with Oriental and Caribbean minorities to the dismay of American Blacks. Liberal repression of unliberal ideas had not been easily overcome. A case in point, Senator Barry Goldwater's *The Conscience of A Conservative* (1960), was a trail-breaker. I went to the source of its story for my purposes here.

"Dear Holmes: [the Senator wrote me] *The Conscience of a Conservative* came about in a rather strange way. Dean Manion of Notre Dame, whom I knew slightly, asked me if I would write a book and I said I would. He offered me $10,000 to do this which in those days to me was the same as a million. I put together my thoughts and sent them to him, and he was not happy with them, so I suggested that I get Brent Bozell to help me out and Brent did.

"Actually the book was written more from speeches that I made in my candidacies and in the Senate than anything else, but it did turn out all right. I don't think that Brent and I ever realized more than $20,000 off the three-and-a-half million copies that were printed, so we didn't do so well on it. But, by golly, conservatism did and, to me, that's the important thing.

"If you'd like to talk any more about this, just come in any time and we can sit down and twist it around. With best wishes. Barry" (signed).

There's more to it than that. Barry had started a newspaper column, much like my own, and it caught on for much the same reasons. Clarence Manion, Dean of Notre Dame Law School, recognized the column's appeal, along with Goldwater's strong and forthright personality. Despairing of finding a major house to bring out a book, Manion arranged with Victor Publishing Company, Shephardsville, Kentucky, for a printing of 10,000 copies. L. Brent Bozell, an established writer, then whipped the volume into shape. This much I knew. But how could such a humbly-born book, author unknown to letters, reach a public, no matter how hungry for the gospel? I phoned Bozell who told me:

"A secretary and I set up shop on Eye Street, N.W., and phoned every bookstore in the country. We said that this new Republican Senator had something to say, gave them each the publisher's address. Then we did the same for every known critic in the land."

After that, it was word of mouth, the best of all promotion systems—"Did you read that Goldwater book?" Fourteen weeks after publication, and after he had made the N.Y. *Times* bestseller list, the *Times* gave Barry a review.

A non-writer with ideas, a discoverable public, and determined backers would do what many a long-suffering scholar could not. Goldwater had crashed the gates. He learned that the American people had been dictatorially excluded from ideas. Thereafter, Goldwater's books came like olives that follow the first one from the bottle. He had no trouble finding publishers after he had found his public.

But the fight for the expression of contrary opinion was uphill all the way. Charles Beard, my old hero, observed in a *Saturday Evening Post* editorial, October 4, 1947, that big money was on the line to corrupt the First Amendment. The Rockefeller Foundation donated $139,000 to the Council on Foreign Relations for the stated purpose of blocking repetition of "the debunking journalistic campaign following World War I." To "debunk" was to disagree with official line. Beard asked, was World War II to be reported only by authors with liberal foundations' approval and money? Why not open the field to all comers?

Beard, joined by Norman Thomas, objected to the release of selected government papers to a certain Harvard professor who guaranteed to give a Roosevelt slant to events between 1938-45. Beard, Thomas and others made enough noise to draw attention to their crusade. The small firm, Devin-Adair (Greenwich, Connecticut), published George Morgenstern's *Pearl Harbor: The Story of the Secret War* (1948). It was a dam-breaker. Thereafter, enough antiestablishment material poured into print to raise this question: Were all the war criminals standing trial at Nuremberg? Should Roosevelt, Marshall and their like stand in the dock?

Taft's presidential chances would be enhanced in '48 if he could rivet attention on the domestic economy. Russia was making that difficult. Taft's ponderous sincerity, especially his Mc-Carthyism, handicapped him. His chief competitors for the GOP nomination were wrapped in the UN banner—Dewey, Vandenberg, Stassen. I thought Taft had an unrealized asset in what was very nearly my personal discovery. Hardly anybody else, least of all any national reporters, knew about Republican Senator George Malone of Nevada. His person, if not his ideology, was visible enough. "Molly" Malone was a chunky outdoorsman, a non-stop talker, a one-time Golden Gloves boxer and a civil engineer. Of most importance, the freshman Senator had former President Herbert Hoover as a close friend and associate. Whatever his political shortcomings, Mr. Hoover was an intense patriot and a world-famous geologist and civil engineer.

Malone, as chairman for the Department of the Interior subcommittee on metals, minerals and materials, showed me a thick file of correspondence with Hoover (whom he addressed as "Chief"). These documents contained vital information, which I guessed would get the brushoff in the exaggerated spirit of internationalism.

Hoover's firm opinion was that North America, probably, and the Western Hemisphere, certainly, could be made substantially self-sufficient in industrial minerals. Such gaps as showed in scanty or low-yield deposits would take time and money to develop, but much less expense than the many foreign aid programs. And we would be investing in our economic independence. Where short supplies of raw materials persisted, we should rely on American ingenuity and technology for synthetic products. Nothing was impossible in science, according to George Malone or Herbert Hoover. Neither lived to see American science triumphant in the space programs.

Senator Malone brought Hoover's information to the 80th Congress, 1947-48, and I wrote it up. Malone and Montana Senator Mike Mansfield helped me to new clients in the Western newspapers. It was a time when such ideas had the highest potential and the lowest acceptability. The international cult looked upon self-sufficiency as isolationism, which it was. Some Senators whom I lobbied for the Malone plan said we'd be richer for hoarding underground wealth instead of developing it. Others declared we must purchase raw materials abroad to bolster our "world leadership." They insisted we were blocking communism by supporting the colonial empires of Britain, France, Belgium and Holland. The coming revolt of the colonized natives simply was not contemplated in the State Departments of Marshall, Acheson, Dulles and Herter.

Meanwhile, U.S. firms and the CIA were wading into Mideast oil and politics. In the short view, petroleum could be imported cheaply, never mind the distances and the risks. In the long view, Hoover-Malone's economics favored explorative investment in the Rocky Mountain states and seabeds. But who would listen? Foreign aid had been evangelically sold to Congress. Big Business of the Eastern states and pseudo-intellectuals of academia considered Malone a galoot.

Malone's subcommittee hearings stretched on into Eisenhower's term (they were golfing partners), but begat no policies. Truthfully, Malone was not a well-regarded Senator. He drank too much. He was ungrammatical. He could empty the Senate floor with a lecture on geology. But Western state newspapers responded to him and his subject, and bought my column. I found weekends and nights to write *Tomorrow's Air Age* (Rinehart, 1953). It dealt with energy, building materials, navigation and medicine in the coming jetplane era. My book won a Doolittle Committee award, translations into French and Italian, sales to *Fortune, Newsweek* (where it was a cover story) and numerous house organs of the aviation industry, with excellent reviews everywhere except the *Washington Post* where it got the Averted Gaze.

The more I traveled, the more nationalistic I became. I made an extensive trip through North Africa and Europe for *Nation's Business* magazine. My assignment was to write up MATS (military air transport service), and I continued my columns en route. Mostly they were about our unfinished bomber bases on the southern rim of the Mediterranean. Upon return I had my first meeting with Senator Lyndon Johnson, chairman of the Preparedness subcommittee.

"Senator, there's a multimillion dollar scandal of military waste growing up in North Africa."

"Cracking down on military waste is like swatting flies," he growled. "No end to it."

"At those building sites, food is thrown into the garbage to increase purchases. The construction work is so poor that a French plane tried to land to celebrate on Bastille Day and got stuck in wet concrete. We don't need overseas bases because we've developed aerial refueling and the coming aircraft have longer range."

The Senator was impatient. "What the hell do you expect me to do about it?"

"You have the power of subpoena to investigate."

I thought I had the well-known brushoff, but shortly afterward Johnson sent his administrative assistant, George Reedy, to interview me. LBJ openly held big hearings (everything with him was big), and he also wrote to editors in Texas and recommended me to their papers. It was a bonanza for the "new girl in town."

I wrote another book, *How to Read the Federalist*. The *Federalist Papers'* principal authors, Hamilton and Madison, were intense nationalists who never went overseas. I had a small publisher (Western Islands) and again was snubbed by the capital city's leading newspaper. The Baltimore *Sun* gave a boost to my book (it went into paperback), but of more significance, the Columbus *Dispatch* in Taft's home state commented on ". . . the interesting style of writing familiar to readers of his column" and declared that the essays in which I tried to popularize the *Federalist* "contain fundamentals that are as sound today as when they were written."

Taft was not alive when the book belatedly appeared (1961), but his ideas were in my columns, as well as in the Senator's stolid campaign addresses across the land. The people agreed with him, but they were not enthralled. Taft promised nothing except good government. What is more dull than virtue?

It was a wild political year, 1948. The Democratic Convention tried to dump Truman, thought to be a sure loser, and to nominate Eisenhower. Radical Democrats bolted to Henry Wallace. Southern Democrats walked out and chose Strom Thurmond. By this time the Republicans had already picked their dandy little efficiency expert, Tom Dewey of New York. He had left Taft eating the bitter dust of defeat.

Governor Dewey seemed such a shoo-in to be the next president that I summoned my wife to Philadelphia to see the ceremonial selection of Truman's assumed successor. We watched from the McNaught press reserved sections as Dewey pranced on stage to polite applause. Some Republican ladies there collared him with a triumphal horseshoe.

I heard Mary murmur that he reminded her of Armed, the horse of the year. I whispered back that Armed was a gelding. That's what she meant, replied Mary, and who could love or vote for a gelding? I shushed her, but she wrote something on my copy paper and sealed it in an envelope marked "Open on Election Day."

I did so on November 4. She had written, "Mr. Truman wins."

13.

The War of Darkness at Home: I

SENATOR BOB TAFT WAS A GOOD LOSER—twice, to inferior statesmen. Shortly after Eisenhower's inauguration in 1953, the Robert Tafts held a reception for the Eisenhowers in their Georgetown home. Mary and I were invited along with some correspondents and all the Republican Senators. The new President and his wife, barely known within his own party, roamed about the modest house. The stricken Martha Taft received from a wheelchair with her stolid full-bellied husband proudly beside her. One GOP leader reverentially knelt to kiss the hostess's hand.

The commanding figure of the gathering—of any gathering—was Alice Roosevelt Longworth, called Princess Alice. This vibrant personality, known at the time for her astonishing hats and acid tongue, was talking with my wife while I hovered nearby. Alice detected Senator Joe McCarthy with his tall, handsome fiancee at some distance across the room. Joe was lifting a highball when Alice in a carrying voice remarked with what became the watchword of anti-McCarthyism:

"I hope it's poison."

Despite my wife's restraining fingers, I went over to speak to Joe, who introduced me to Jean Kerr, a strict Presbyterian who was known to be taking Catholic instructions to marry into Mc-Carthy's church.

"Now, why would that nice old lady say a thing like that?" he laughed.

Long before the Taft reception I had come to know Joe, who insisted on the first name usage. After attending some of his rough-on-Reds hearings (Jack Kennedy was saying that "Joe's got something" and Bob Kennedy was a committee counsel) I arranged through the Republican National Committee for a McCarthy interview.

It would have been simpler to phone for an appointment, as McCarthy was notably accessible, but I preferred an official introduction so as to avoid any obligation. I reminded my contact at the GOP committee, Ab Hermann (once a Boston Braves third baseman) that I had been writing adversely about the Wisconsin Senator and chose not to meet him under any misunderstandings. Hermann made the engagement with that preamble which I repeated as soon as I reached Joe's private office.

"Senator, it's only fair to say that I'm against you."

McCarthy was a hairy-armed "black" Irishman, still a bachelor and Jack Kennedy's closest rival as a Senatorial womanizer. Joe responded to my opener with a friendly guffaw.

"Why, that's okay with me," he said. "What's one more writer jumping on my neck? Tell me your beef."

"Just that you're smearing your witnesses without any evidence against them."

He guffawed again with amiable amusement, and asked me to give an example. I named a name.

"Well, let's see about that guy," said Joe. He rang for a secretary who brought him a file on the man I'd named, and opened the folder before me. It showed the abused witness to have membership in numerous organizations for "peace," brotherhood, world harmony and such; nearly all the groups were listed by the Justice Department as suspect if not subversive.

"Guilt by association," I said. "It proves nothing."

"Nope," said McCarthy. "It doesn't. But is this the sort of jerk you want in the State Department? Hell, I could subpoena Earl Browder and nail him as a commie, but what for? Somebody's got to dig out these slinky bastards who aren't in the open. I'll tell you this. Bob Taft, Bill Knowland, Styles Bridges and a lot of senior Republicans, as well as military intelligence and the FBI send names through that door where you came in. They say, 'We don't want to touch this fellow, but you do it, Joe. Your hands are already bloody.'"

After that, I took him more seriously, but not entirely so. Joe's infamous speech at Wheeling where he charged that an elastic number of known communists worked at the State Department was not of his own research. The original figure, 205, was handed him by the Chicago *Tribune* Senate correspondent who needed a quotable source to avoid libel. Similar material came to McCarthy from a House Un-American Activities committee report. The numbers were garbled and government-wide, but not fabricated. Espionage cases were in the courts and proliferating: Amerasia, Gouzenko, Coplon, Wadleigh, Fuchs, Hiss, Service et. al. The Acheson biographer McClellan wrote, "It is quite conceivable that McCarthy really believed" his accusations. It is certain that, as a few writers conceded, he was a black-and-white thinker who was as outraged as the large following of average Americans he initially attracted. He was far from being the first Red-baiter in public life.

Foul and irrational tactics by Joe's opponents kindled my sympathy. At the time I had no newspaper clients in Wisconsin which might have made for pro-or-con influence. His enraged enemies more than equaled him in blackguardism. I read that "documents" existed to prove Joe a "crypto-Jew" and name-changer, a shopworn bid for anti-Semitism. The Fascist insult became current. I interviewed Senator Bill Fulbright who said, "He makes me think of Hitler." I hadn't the gall to ask Fulbright, who insincerely filibustered himself hoarse in support of White Supremacy to keep his Senate seat, if he meant Hitler the racist? Joe's only bigotry in color was Red. Did Fulbright mean Hitler the fearsome dictator? Joe was not even a precinct political boss in Wisconsin.

More than a few entrenched foreign service officers told me that McCarthy was a secret communist with the mission of undermining the American reputation abroad. Both the *New York Times* and the *Times* of London came out to say that he'd "conquered" the U.S. Army. A Baltimore lady, who admitted she'd never seen the man, declared him a queer. These were days when homosexuals were still in the closet, but I surmise the lady had been reading such innuendo as this by a *New Yorker* author:

"Many people were firmly convinced that he was a homosexual. The evidence was wholly circumstantial. . . . a member of his staff was picked up in LaFayette Park as a sodomist. . . . A Marquette coed was anonymously quoted as saying that Joe's lovemaking was merely 'verbal'."

After putting the slurs into print, the author admitted he had "no data at all."

My sympathies for Joe and Jean were built up by this leftwing McCarthyism, and also because he had a certain shaggy dog appeal. There was a fugitive hurt beneath his uncouth bluster. To me, his best character witness would always be Jean, who married him, but only after arranging with FBI Director J. Edgar Hoover for a rival temptress to be assigned to Alaska.

As Joe's researcher, Jean had a hand in faking a photograph of Senator Tydings in a closeup with communist Earl Browder. Asked if this constituted falsehood, Jean insisted that the picture truthfully represented Chairman Tydings's friendliness to the communist witness.

Long after McCarthy's death when Jean had remarried and I hadn't seen her for several years, she phoned my office to thank me for a paragraph from my book, *Pen and Politics*, which carried a sympathetic paragraph about her loyalty to Joe. She invited my wife and me to dinner with her new husband, a Democratic civil servant, provided that we would keep the conversation off the past. The invitation was never consumated because, as I think we both felt, the conditions she imposed were impossible.

I had thought much and even attempted a novel about the Jean and Joe story. I came to see the tragi-romantic yarn as a variation of the Dorian Gray and Pygmalion themes. The portrait of Joe as developed by cartoonists and writers during his five tumultous years of notoriety was typically one of the stubbled, dissipated, leering, slime-covered beast from the sewers. With artistic allowance for caricature, the picture was heartless but not inaccurate or truly unjust, and Jean would weep disconsolately over it. She couldn't help but remember the dark, rugged, energetic Irish northwesterner into whose Senate office suite she had walked as a coed on the hunt for a 1947 summer job.

This willowy, blue-eyed beauty, a prize-winning essayist on "Promotion and Peace," elected Cherry Blossom Queen and prettiest-in-the-class, a cum laude journalism student, had dropped in to pick up a girl companion and did not accept the instant offer of a job which Joe relayed. Perhaps his wolfish reputation warned her off. Instead, she found a related position with a Senate special investigating panel. Eventually, after work in an advertising agency and graduating from academic courses at Northwestern and George Washington Universities, she became an assistant researcher for McCarthy.

Comely and popular "Jeannie," Washington-born of a Scotch-born immigrant housebuilder, had been mainly interested in her college electives on political science, with journalism for purposes of salary. She was soon teaching her employer about the communist policy of world conquest by war and subversion, of which he was at first profoundly ignorant.

Capitol Hill gossip mills certainly informed Jean of the worst about this freshman Senator, who had upset young Bob La Follette in '46. An ambitious and unscrupulous poor boy, Joe rushed through an education, coached boxing, won a circuit judgeship by unethical campaign tricks, phonied a Marine Corps record as a Pacific Island ground officer to become "Machine Gunner Joe" in the electioneering slogan. Settled in Washington, he became a social drinker and lusty bachelor.

As a female Pygmalion, Jean found him an eager and attractive model for a scourge against communism, against Soviet world conquest by war and subversion. They drove to the Maryland farm of Whittaker Chambers for lectures from the master, cultivated FBI Director Hoover and other conspiratorial types. The female Pygmalion too quickly lost control of her creation, a fact she privately but never publicly acknowledged. Meanwhile Joe's excesses as a ruthless workaholic and the other kind, progressively made his features and body gross and coarsened his manners and menacing sing-song growl on the Senate floor and in committees. He undeniably came more and more to resemble the Dorian Gray portrait in the attic.

Their wedding, September 29, 1953, blessed by a cablegram from the Pope and a personal letter from the President, was an event of the season. The groom was a second-termer at 45, and she in the bloom of life at 29, his brother Bill the best man. St. Matthews Cathedral bulged to a capacity that would not be matched until President Kennedy's funeral a decade later. But the Massachusetts Senator attended the nuptials, as did the Vice President and Pat Nixon, Princess Alice Longworth, Jack Dempsey, CIA Director Allen Dulles, General Persons and Sherman Adams of the White House staff, Jack Martin, who represented the cancer-stricken Senator Taft.

Some 3,500 onlookers thronged Rhode Island Avenue. The couple drove off in a deluxe Cadillac, the gift of wealthy Texans and reportedly of 2,000 small contributors to "the most beloved man in America," according to the Texas sponsor. After a brief Caribbean honeymoon, the fortunate pair took up residence in a new air-conditioned Capitol Hill home, given by the bride's delighted mother, of whom Joe was forever fond.

I went several times by invitation to this house, convenient to Union Station, sometimes with my wife and schoolage daughter, my summer helper. Jean was her striking self as hostess, who discussed no politics, and Joe proved an hilarious raconteur in Irish, Swedish, German, Negro and Chinese dialects which he had learned as a hashslinger and dishwasher in these ethnic restaurants during summer recesses. He served drinks, but I never saw him take one while entertaining. (He would stoke himself with vodka and whiskey while at work.) I followed his career only casually in those days of the Korean War winddown, the Suez Canal takeover by Egypt, the Hungarian revolution and the relative peace and prosperity of the Eisenhower era.

Any observer could see that the wild-riding McCarthy was headed for a fall. Not many credited him as a zealot who, by whatever chance, had happened upon the terminal threat to American longevity. Much less was he allowed any margin of error or discounted for atrocious manners in the Senate which had seen noble figures but also more than a few drunkards and galoots like Huey Long.

One day there shuffled into his hearing room a small black woman, an obscure government clerk. Joe officiously rustled among his papers. I hadn't a doubt that he had done little or no research on Annie Lee Moss, who'd somehow appeared on one of his blacklists.

Chairman McCarthy liked witnesses who either cringed or hollered back, and he seemed embarrassed at facing this passive, pathetic-looking creature. He did not detain her long, but the covering press had a tearjerker—this scowling bully towering over the flotsam of a race with centuries of suffering.

Of course, Joe had no more to do with the once "peculiar institution" of slavery than with the licenses for witchhunting under which he operated. The Truman "loyalty" program of 1947 allowed firing government employees of dubious loyalty. An extension of the regulation in 1951 permitted dismissal for "reasonable doubt." President Eisenhower went further by including "security risks" for removal, and the hit list under Ike mounted into four digits. The legislative counterparts of these executive fiats never bore McCarthy's name or authorship. McCarran, Smith, Mundt and Nixon composed the acts that allowed Joe to become the ruthless hunter. He was blamed for spreading a "reign of terror," but he had no storm troopers except his office staff. The fear he instilled never spoke well to me about the courage of two presidents, several cabinet officers and academic institutions which he allegedly terrorized.

Henry Regnery, the "dissident publisher," wrote in 1979:

The McCarthy episode, one of those overblown American phenomena that the communications apparatus periodically produce[s], had reached its climax. The liberal press would have had us believe that the country was in the grip of a wave of terror, the universities in a state of panic, the foreign service paralyzed, books publicly burned, the press about to be stilled—all because of a United States Senator, acting virtually alone. . . . The liberal intellectual establishment gloried in the persecution to which it imagined it was being subjected, and in its own heroism. . . . The fact that it was far more dangerous for a professor to defend McCarthy than to attack him bothered the liberals not at all; . . . . After it had recovered from the shock of his first attack and its own sense of guilt—McCarthy's accusations were by no means without foundation—the establishment proceeded to mobilize its forces and relentlessly to destroy him.

Joe wouldn't be alive four years later, when another investigation found Annie Lee Moss to be "an active member of the Communist party," a courier of propaganda and secret information. Joe-baiters, unwilling to yield him any point, contended that there were two or more persons named Annie Lee Moss, and that it was a case of mistaken identity.

Perhaps this was so. In Shakespeare's *Julius Caesar* the revolutionary mob mistakes Cinna the Poet for Cinna the Conspirator. It could easily happen that way in the melodrama of McCarthy's day. The country was in the initial stages of war fever, World War III, simultaneously was suffering from war sickness, World War II with its Hiroshima shock. Still a third disease, said to be fatal, was cited in the writings of the time by James Burnham. Here Burnham is quoting a learned man of India:

"A civilization is dying," declared this savant in Burnham's introduction to *The Secret War For The A-Bomb* by Medford Evans, "if it is unable to accept the logical consequences of its own inner nature. Now the atomic bomb is . . . a logical and inevitable outcome of two of the innermost, essential features of Western culture: mathematico-empirical science and industrial technology. . . . Confronting this brilliant and wholly legitimate offspring, the spokesmen and leaders of the West, turning their eyes away, trying to deny and avoid it. They feel a sterilizing conviction of guilt instead of a normal sense of achievement, triumph and power. Instead of the hope that ought to spring from the knowledge that they have unlocked the incomparable resources of nuclear energy, they tremble with defeat at their own capacity. . . ."

Little would Joe have understood of such highbrow cogitation, but he had an intuition which took him close to the same conclusions. America lacked the toughness to live up to its postwar challenges and potentials. Somewhere, much earlier in the McCarthyite half-decade than is generally allowed, Joe had become aware of his mission. It was not an intellectual awakening, but a visceral message. Before that, he had reveled in his notoriety and enjoyed all that it brought him—speaking invitations, police escorts, association with monied and learned persons.

As he came to understand, however dimly, the seriousness of

his involvement—the significance of the Cause which was thrust upon him—Joe lost his robust callousness. He became supersensitive. He winced at being "misunderstood" by persons whose admiration he coveted. He was already a problem drinker in Congress where alcoholic excess has become a recognized occupational affliction. His weakness for the bottle fed his self-pity and his stubbornness.

Most of Joe's "victims" were nonentities, whose heads were lopped off by Secretaries Acheson and Dulles, though Joe was blamed. He often went gunning for bigger game. Senators Benton, Lucas and MacFarland have been mentioned as trophies of his manhunts, but none compared with Senator Millard Tydings of Maryland whose fall was Miltonic in its grand pathos.

I had a closeup view of this celebrated case from several angles. Living then in Baltimore, I first gave attention to Owen Lattimore, director of the Walter Hines Page School of International Relations at Johns Hopkins University, a state department consultant. Lattimore was also a regular contributor to the magazine *Amerasia* which took an indistinct Red China line.

Joe had named Lattimore as his prize exhibit of Reds-in-government. I needed to learn what I could of the accused, on whom my jury was still out. Several Sunday afternoons found me interviewing at the suburban home of Dr. and Mrs. Lattimore, and I sometimes met him on Saturdays at his Hopkins campus office.

Seldom, I think, was the inscrutable East so reflected in the flat yellow face and impenetrable demeanor of this Orientalist (he was British-born). I am no better than average as a quiz-reporter; what I learned from the secretive professor was zero. He was not a winsome personality. His pieces in *Amerasia* were subtly slanted, if at all. My inclination was to dismiss prejudicial and circumstantial suspicions. I had published some essays on the *Federalist Papers* in *American Opinion*, a Birchite magazine, but I was a Hamiltonian, not a Bircher; I had written fiction for *Elks Magazine* without being a member of the Elks. Pressing my inquiry, I attended a Hopkins faculty cocktail party, waited until the martinis seemed apt to speak for the guests, and then asked a high-up of JHU: "How do you read Owen Lattimore?"

"Well, I'd gladly trade him for a good lacrosse player," he answered.

I had much better contacts with the tall, militant, articulate Millard Tydings, who would hear Lattimore before a Foreign Relations subcommittee. He was a baron of the upper chamber. He was a fourth-termer and a monumental figure at home. He was a family friend to me. We had been Democratic campaigners when I ran for the legislature in 1930; I had attended his step-daughter's wedding; I last saw him at my father's graveside. No Senator in 1950 had higher committee assignments in the 81st Congress (1949–50)—chairman of Armed Services, high ranker in Foreign Relations, on the Joint Committee on Atomic Energy and one of a half-dozen unofficial watchdogs of the hidden CIA appropriations.

Long before turning columnist I had written (1938) a Tydings profile article for the book, *The American Politician*. I knew him so favorably and intimately that I wished him a safe distance from the contagion of McCarthyism and the enigmatic Lattimore. With an election coming up in 1950, Tydings was loud and sarcastic about the Reds in government. He despised McCarthy; he felt protective toward Lattimore, a Maryland resident. He would need Olympian objectivity to act as an impartial chairman.

At some risk of being presumptuous, I wrote Tydings a note. I told him that he was getting on the wrong side of an undeclared war with the Soviet Union. I pointed out that Senator Lodge, whose fine instincts and patriotism stood above any doubt, had taken a neutral ground. Tydings wrote back in hot haste. Lodge, he said, was "a smart politician" in a Catholic state where McCarthy was strong. For himself, the proud-as-Lucifer Marylander would stand by the Red, White and Blue ideals of fair play and free speech.

Working at home in Baltimore one morning, I took a phone call from his Washington office asking me to come there as soon as possible. Hoping for a scoop I jumped the next train. He said, "Last night at College Park we held a meeting of the Leading Democrats of Maryland. We canvassed names for my reelection campaign manager in publicity, and you're it."

I was pleased but aghast. "Senator, a journalist's got to be a political eunuch. You'll get my vote and support, but I can't work for your campaign. However, I've got some more advice."

"Shoot."

What I wanted most to say was too indelicate. Long a sought-after bachelor, Tydings had married money, bought a large estate on the Susquehanna River, gone in for Washington society. What I did say was: "You're out of touch with the Maryland people. Your private driveway is two miles off the main road. If your campaign gets controversial, you'll be vulnerable."

"Everybody knows me, and what I stand for."

"The people aren't sure they still know you. Show yourself in the streets and barbershops. Stand up at Rotary and Kiwanis and Veterans clubs. You may not know it, but you're in for trouble."

"Roosevelt tried to purge me in '38, didn't he?"

He could see no danger from McCarthy and the rightwing. I repeated that the real danger was that the Maryland people no longer knew him.

Tydings scoffed. "Why, last weekend I drove all the way down from Allegheny county to the southern end of Charles county."

He didn't realize that merely cruising the Maryland towns wasn't enough. He thought of himself as a Southern conservative Democrat, strong within the coalition that ruled the Senate. He held himself to be above competition.

His arrogance was appalling. I was at the press table of the Senate Caucus Room when Lattimore read his statement to the subcommittee. He'd been welcomed by the chairman and invited in heavy humor to disprove McCarthy's charges of being the "head Red spy." A cheering section from Johns Hopkins volleyed applause when Lattimore finished his prepared denials. Tydings sat grinning and did not rap for order until the demonstration subsided.

Later, in a still more shocking burst of poor taste, Tydings took the Senate floor and boasted of an ancient medal from yesteryear's war. Jenner of Indiana, an ardent McCarthyite, rose to answer that Tydings was now serving Joseph Stalin.

"I have another medal for the distinguished Senator from Maryland," shouted Jenner. "It is inscribed *Well done, from Old Joe.*"

I hurried to Tydings' office. He had been known in the past for hot temper and free fists.

"You ought to take a swing at Jenner."

"Well, no, but the next time he runs, I'll go to Indiana and speak against him."

By that time Tydings was a humiliated ex-Senator, beaten for a fifth term in what he considered a lifetime seat. He was undone by McCarthy smear tactics in what the Senate elections and privileged committee dubbed "a despicable backstreet campaign." It was all of that. My column sadly observed that all politicians are volunteers, and should not complain of gunfire.

I could have carried the military allusion a little further. The country was being awakened to the rumbles of World War III, and in its fever was hearing anti-communism in the bugle call. Only in such a madhouse melee could Tydings have been unhorsed, but there he lay.

It was not so much the Age of McCarthyism. It was the Age of Insanity.

14.

The War of Darkness at Home: II

ALL OF US WHO LIVED through the American Dark Decades 1950–80 (and more so those who were Washington reporters) still find it hard to believe all that happened.

We left an unwon war at the DMZ in Korea, and retreated from a lost one off the embassy roof at Saigon in Vietnam. We allowed a vice president and then a president to say, "Sorry about that" and walk away from their crimes while their accomplices paid the penalties.

We lived, we citizens of a proud republic, under a nonelected ruler, and permitted him to give an open-end pardon to the culprit who had appointed him. It was a time of assassinations and street disorders, of burning cities and shameful concessions to foreign adversaries. We paid a ransom to the mini-powers in Cuba and Iran, while dropping from world supremacy into the international netherlands.

We hadn't quite forgotten to boast of our democracy. Any American boy could grow up to be president. Dick, Spiro, Gerry and Jimmy convinced us that this grand opportunity, while a bonanza in perks, pensions, royalties and lecture fees, is one of democracy's flaws.

The Englishman Bryce had planted the notion that we preferred second-raters in the most powerful office on earth. The Frenchman Tocqueville, writing in and of the Andrew Jackson Era, found that "equality" fostered tyranny by minority groups at home. His clairvoyance about America and Russia in their foreign affairs was inexplicable genius. Although well-known to scholars, it demands citation in any study of America's Dark Decades. Tocqueville wrote:

"There are at the present time two great nations in the world, which started from different points, but seem to tend toward the same end. I allude to the Russians and the Americans. Both of them have grown up unnoticed; and whilst the attention of mankind was directed elsewhere, they have suddenly placed themselves in the front rank . . . to sway the destinies of half the globe."

Stalin, writing in 1947, updated Tocqueville: "The existence of the Soviet Republic side by side with capitalistic states for a long time is unthinkable. One or the other must triumph in the end."

Neither of the empires had been obtained with immaculate hands. Americans had taken their continent as much by the long rifle as by "the plowshare." The nature of "morality" in warfare remains undefined, and the activities of McCarthy, and much darker ones of the CIA, do not lift us above mankind. General William T. Sherman is still the best authority on the hellishness of human conflict which does not spare the bystanders. Civilians get killed in the clash of armies; senators and generals in Joe McCarthy's swath did not escape the tongue-lash. Symington was Sanctimonious Stu, Fulbright was Halfbright, Benton a mental midget, Flanders "senile," General Ralph Zwicker "a disgrace to the uniform."

Joe's vituperation, though uncouth and graceless, was not without its counterpart in our political history. Alexander Hamilton, Randolph of Roanoke, Andrew Jackson, Henry Clay, to mention some, all fought duels over written or spoken insults. In another day, Joe might have answered to the Code Duello. Less forthright means were long explored to bring him down—recall motions, cancellation of his committee memberships, investigation of his finances, removal from the White House invitation list, all leading toward the eventual censure.

Madman he may have seemed; if so, he raged in a mad world of creeping disaster for America and the West. Some sane and patriotic men suspended judgment. Senator Paul Douglas, genuine Marine hero, liberal and intellectual, never joined the two-party protest. Arthur Watkins, later the chairman of censorship, did not raise his voice. Robert Taft had openly encouraged Joe. Bill Buckley, young paladin of the Right, believed "McCarthyism ... is a movement around which men of goodwill and stern morality can close ranks." Buckley's co-author and brother-in-law, L. Brent Bozell, joined the McCarthy staff in a stablilizing effort. None of the above is explicable save that the antis thought civil liberty and decorum were endangered, while the cons were alert to the communist march and knew in their hearts that Joe was no nervous shepherd boy shouting "Wolf! Wolf!"

Revisionist history, tracing the footsteps of Mencken, Beard and Lindbergh, was also taking shape. At Georgetown University two professors of the revisionist school were accumulating ammunition for a volley which Joe would fire at an American idol—General George C. Marshall. Forrest Davis, a *Saturday Evening Post* article writer, became a ghost writer for Joe and other rightwing causes.

The theme of Professors Charles Tansill and Stefan Possony, by now an axiom but startling in 1951, was that Soviet Russia was stealing a lead over America in the arms-and-influence race. These academics were no crackpots; their credentials of scholarship were in order. In 1936, Tansill's *America Goes to War* (Little Brown) was called "absolutely indispensable" by Allan Nevins, and by Henry Steel Commager "one of the notable achievements of scholarship of this generation." Nonetheless, Tansill's postwar book, *Backdoor to War* had to find a small new publisher, Henry Regnery of Chicago. Stefan Possony, Tansill's top-notch co-author, became another Regnery author with *A Century of Conflict*, an anti-Establishment work. In the most factual study on McCarthy at the time, Buckley and Bozell produced *McCarthy and His Enemies* (1954). They found, as I did, "McCarthy deserved to be censored." They agreed his case against the State Department was "neither full nor fair." Still, an examination of disastrous U.S. foreign policy was overdue, and in the prevailing atmosphere could not be gently done.

The big lie technique (sometimes called "multiple untruth") was waged by both sides. McCarthy's charges were rebutted by the slogan, "He never caught a communist," but unless the word is pedantically defined, he "caught" hundreds, including Lattimore, whom a Senate select committee of former state attorneys general declared to be "a conscious articulate instrument of the communist conspiracy." Walter Goodman's *The Committee* (1962) (on Un-American Activities) is left-leaning but not unfair. Goodman concluded in retrospect:

"The Bentley and Chambers testimony taken together tended to show, not that there was a widespread network of subversives in Washington during the thirties and forties, but that [American] communists, at the height of their prestige, had succeeded in planting a handful of their own in government."

Is a discovered "handful" insignificant? Had U.S. foreign policy under FDR been subverted? If there were any question, General Marshall was the logical person to answer for it. He'd had an unbelievable memory lapse about the Sunday of Pearl Harbor. While so much was going wrong, Marshall had been Army Chief of Staff, White House advisor, Secretary of State and of Defense, special emissary to China where he favored an impossible coalition of Left and Right. Richard Rovere felt compelled to admit:

"There is a case to be made against George Marshall; like a great many Americans of his time, he was unprepared to see, as Winston Churchill for one could see, beyond the immediate conflict with fascism to the developing conflict with the Soviet Union and Communist China. This is only to say that, while he served the republic well, he served it with somewhat less foresight than one can with hindsight, which he—and with him most of our warleaders—had shown."

In justice to Marshall, he had larger and deeper understanding of world warfare than many of our other war leaders. His defenders against McCarthy—Jenner, Taft and others of the rightwing—would have made a far better case for the General had they relied on (in all probability they had not read) Marshall's cogent, 123-page volume.

Marshall's work (1947) was a staff paper to the War Department under the cumbersome title "The Winning of the War in Europe and the Pacific: Biennial Report of the Chief of Staff of the U.S. Army, 1943–1945." Its author, like Wilson, Franklin Roosevelt and other American militarist-statesmen, did not have an historian's comprehension (as, for instance, had Charles Beard) of the intricate ethnical politics of Europe, much less of Asia. Marshall's advantage over these men was that he did not reach beyond his grasp. His small book confined itself to what he knew, and it is valuable for that reason.

Basically, Marshall was in line with the thinking of the Founders. He advocated universal military training as a means of preparedness without a standing army. Being ready for war as a means of preventing war meant to Marshall a large weapons industry which, he said, would be worthless unless the war-machine had access to trained manpower to operate them. He wrote in part:

"We have tried since the birth of our nation to promote our love of peace by a display of weakness. This course has failed us utterly, cost us millions of lives and billions of treasure. The reasons are quite understandable. The world does not seriously regard the desires of the weak. Weakness presents too great a temptation to the strong. . . . We must, if we are to realize the hopes that we may now dare for a lasting peace, reinforce our will for peace with strength. We must make it clear to the potential gangsters of the world that if they dare break our peace they will do so at their great peril. . . ."

He went on to discuss the atomic bomb and the "conventional" weapons with their long range and deadly heat-seeking accuracy. To rely overly on the technocracy—he called it "the machine power"—is negative defense, as demonstrated by the Maginot Line. The only feasible offensive defense is "men to man the machines . . . men to come to close grips with the enemy and tear his operating bases and his productive establishment away from him before the war can end."

This Marshall demonstrated by Britain's plight under the Nazi V-bombs which did not cease to fall until Allied armies crossed the channel and "had physical possession of the launching sites and the factories. . . ." Marshall closed his book by a paraphrase of George Washington's familiar warning: ". . . if we desire to avoid insult we must be ready to repel it; if we desire to secure peace . . . it must be known that we are at all times ready for war."

And ready for peace? By 1947 this worried Marshall into a

prophetic mood which he expressed in a Washington's Birthday address at Princeton University:

"The war years were critical, at times alarmingly so. But I think the present period is, in many respects, even more critical. . . . we no longer display that intensity of purpose with which we concentrated on war tasks and achieved the victory."

I allot this considerable space to Marshall's writing, because it is hardly known and because it deserves to be placed in advance of what comes next.

McCarthy was not one to see the fine points. Hindsight to him did not cure statesmen of calamity. One of the finest points in the Constitution is the definition of treason, the only crime there described. Joe found it much easier to cry conspiracy, which he equated with treason. On June 13, 1951, he took the Senate floor to assault Marshall with the material of Tansill-Possony-Davis.

From the press gallery, I thought it an unimpressive show. Joe undertook a 200-page, 60,000-word philippic against the nation's most respected soldier-statesman. He didn't pretend to have composed it. He delivered it only in part before receiving "unanimous" consent from a near-empty floor to have his diatribe printed in the Congressional Record.

In preparation for this memoir, I went to the Senate Library in 1980, machine-copied and restudied the speech—which it hardly was. It was a prosecutor's case against the decision-makers in the nation's decline from power, which, even in 1951, was ominous. Joe's address was a follow-on to the Senate hearings on the MacArthur dismissal. For McCarthy's purposes every strategic and diplomatic miscalculation had the appearance of treachery—not invading the Balkans to keep Russia out of Eastern Europe, negotiating Russia into the war against Japan, not insisting on a Berlin corridor.

By choosing lurid passages, an anti-McCarthy biographer could make him a degenerate character assassin. Marshall was "a man so steeped in falsehood . . . who has recourse to the lie whenever it suits his convenience. . . . [a member of] a conspiracy so immense and an infamy so black as to dwarf any previous venture in the history of man. . . . a pattern which finds his

decision maintained with great stubborness and skill, always and
invaribly serving the word policy of the Kremlin."

But if studied after the cooling off of three decades, Joe's hefty
document seems not one to be scornfully dismissed. Signifi-
cantly, it is titled *America's Retreat From Victory*. Twenty-two years
after its delivery, the eminent British journalist Henry Brandon
published *Retreat of American Power*. Similar titles—identical
themes. Objectively, it could be said that Joe got there fustest
with the mostest.

Soon afterwards General Marshall, in pain from a radical
kidney operation, went into permanent retirement at his attractive country home in Leesburg, Virginia. He regularly reviewed
the uniformed graduates of Foxcroft School, Middleburg, having arranged for West Point to supply manuals on drill and
dress for his close friend, Headmistress Charlotte Noland. My
daughter was a Foxcroft student and graduate, so that I met
the soldier-statesman in pleasant circumstances. Despite his
modest demeanor and reputation, I never quite believed the
legend that he unwillingly accepted so many topmost political
appointments.

Much less, and with no intent at debunkery, did I accept other
laurels hung upon him. Before his death at 79 in 1959, Marshall
would be likened in print to his "fellow Virginian Robert E. Lee,"
who commanded great armies in the field. Marshall was born on
December 31, 1880, in Uniontown, Pennsylvania, son of a pros-
perous merchant of that anthracite coal region and the adversary of the organizing Labor forces. The family background was
borderstate Kentucky, and the senior Marshall's only Civil War
combat was in a skirmish as a town militiaman and a surrendered
prisoner to a Union force. The younger Marshall, as well as his
brother, attended private school before going to the Virginia
Military Institute. At VMI senior cadets spoke with disdain of his
"appalling Pittsburgh twang," which admiring writers later
found to be a soft "southern accent." The northern voice intensified his hazing, and the wretched Pennsylvania boy was sen-
tenced to crouch naked for ten minutes over an upright bayonet.
Marshall, weakened by a bout of typhoid, collapsed upon the
steel and suffered a gushing wound variously reported as in the

groin or buttocks. Lifelong stoic that he was, Marshall neither complained or explained, and his biographers never knew (or never told) whether the injury was related to two childless marriages.

Tragically, his first wife, Lily Carter, a belle of Lexington, revealed on the honeymoon that she had a heart condition which would render her a wife in name only. For 26 years, until Lily's death from a heart attack, Marshall endured a silent martyrdom. He was seldom photographed as smiling, although his remarriage to a widow with three children was placid and happy. Many women found him extraordinarily attractive, including London court figures in his long stay abroad after the First World War, and in later years the vivacious Queen Fredericka of Greece and the scheming Madame Chiang Kai-shek. Yet no breath of scandal blew across his long, widely-traveled life.

The General declined lucrative offers to write his Second World War memoirs, as virtually all his contemporaries were doing. His reticence was variously interpreted as unwillingness to bare personal matters, his amnesia about where he was on the unforgettable Pearl Harbor weekend, a disinclination to criticize his fellow-officers in the military or his associates in political administrations. His publicity-shyness invariably keynoted the explanations.

However, to complete the record, it should be noted that Marshall, as a Pershing staff officer, wrote *Memoirs of My Services in the World War, 1917–18*. It was not, as often reported, voluntarily withheld from readership, but rejected (writes biographer Leonard Mosley) because "U.S. publishers were finding no market for wartime reminiscences" in the mid-1920s. The book was published in 1976 by Houghton Mifflin.

Marshall, in 1956–57, gave a series of thirteen known tape-recordings to his "official biographer," Forrest C. Pogue, director of the Research Center, George C. Marshall Foundation, with the editorial assistance of Gordon Harrison. General Omar Bradley wrote the Foreword and the multi-volume work was launched in 1963 by Viking Press, with a portion of the royalties to revert to the Foundation.

* * *

Far from being ostracized by his party, McCarthy was a smash hit at the GOP convention of '52 which nominated Eisenhower. He was in demand around the campaign circuit and won reelection by a reduced but substantial majority. However, the seeds of his demise had been planted back in 1950, with Republican Senator Margaret Smith's "Declaration of Conscience," cosigned by five other Republicans. The seeds were nurtured by Joe's headlong encounters with Ike's appointees and Army personnel. He did not, of course, achieve (to quote the *Times* of London) "what General Burgoyne and General Cornwallis never achieved—the surrender of the American Army." This was a typical European extravagance plagiarized from the hate-Joe American press.

The McCarthy-Army hearings, avidly followed for three months on television, did much to bring about his overthrow in December 1954, an off-shoot of presidential politics.

At that time three contenders for the next White House vacancy (presuming Ike's exit after a second term) were jockeying for position. Senator Jack Kennedy was conveniently in Palm Beach recuperating from serious back surgery. Lyndon Johnson, Senate Majority Floor Leader, "minded the store." He meant to earn the 1960 nomination by proving himself master of his party in the upper chamber. He needed to corral all the Democratic votes for the projected censure, especially Jack Kennedy's. The ambitious Massachusetts Senator was in a cleft stick. He didn't want to vote against McCarthy because of the Catholics in the Bay State and elsewhere. His father and bankroller, Ambassador Joseph Kennedy, was a McCarthy addict. In these circumstances, Jack Kennedy "called in sick," the only Democrat who managed not to vote for or against Joe. "That boy," Johnson told me sarcastically, "just couldn't find a telephone or telegraph station in all Palm Beach.

A third White House seeker, along with Kennedy and Johnson, was Vice-President Nixon. In theory, the vice-president, as president of the Senate, names Senate select committees which represent neither party, but the entire membership. The key figure of a select committee is its chairman and presiding officer.

Whether the choice was made by Nixon alone, or in a deal with LBJ, I never learned.

Senator Arthur Watkins of Utah, frail and timid in appearance, was fortified with an unbending Morman conscience. The liberal press credited Watkins with "white face courage" in gaveling McCarthy into order, but Watkins had earlier given me a clue to his steadfastness in the chair. In explaining why he could not support any foreign aid bill which went to finance Britain, Watkins said to me, "My Church believes there must never again be any monarch in America."

He may have found Joe a tyrannical personality, although it was a late discovery. In any event the Chairman was impeccably dutiful, and the staunchness cost him the loss of his Senate seat in the next election. The select committee could not have functioned without his firm control. This was the essential issue, Senate Resolution 301 (by Flanders):

"Resolved, that the conduct of the Senator from Wisconsin, Mr. McCarthy, is unbecoming a member of the United States Senate, is contrary to Senate traditions, and tends to bring the Senate into disrepute."

There was an eleventh hour chance of reprieve. Barry Goldwater told me that he and Edward Bennett Williams went to see Joe by night in the hospital and showed him the draft of a mild disclaimer. If Joe would sign, these GOP leaders had assurances that the resolution would be tabled. Joe violently rejected this tender by good friends. He scorned retreat, much less surrender.

Only twenty-two Republicans, half the GOP membership, voted against the resolution. In all, sixty-seven Senators, or two-thirds, voted for it. The outcome was not unexpected, but to Joe it signaled a repulse at the enemy's ramparts. It made little difference that Nixon managed to have McCarthy "condemned" rather than censured. Like the Spartan youth with the fox under the cloak, Joe did not cry aloud. With Jean, with more intimate friends than I, he wept bitterly. Long a heavy drinker and warned that alcohol would kill him, he reached for it as a form of hemlock.

Joe had fought without quarter, and he received none in return. Liberals attempted to block Joe's and Jean's planned adoption of a child from the New York Foundling Home. After his death, they tried to wrench the infant from the widow. Cardinal Spellman rode to their rescue, and in January 1957 the daughter was named Tierney Elizabeth for the two mothers of the foster parents. By this time, Joe was nearing his end, which came May 2, 1957.

Too much, I suppose, can be made of coincidental symbolism, but by this date the country had slipped into a ditch from which it has not yet ascended. Taft was dead of cancer, Eisenhower's term had proved no renaissance, McCarthy died in the same Bethesda Naval Hospital where a decade before, another unreasoning communist fighter, James Forrestal, had plunged to death.

Not until 1982 would the country have the benefit of an objective McCarthy biography in an 800-page in-depth study by Professor Thomas C. Reeves (U. of Wisconsin-Parkside). The book achieves the fugitive grace of objectivity, always preferable to polemics. Unblinking toward Joe's faults, it ends on the summary:

"Still, Joe had many personal qualities that biographers and others have chosen to ignore. He was not the amoral, cynical, thieving, homosexual monster his critics described. . . .

"From any standpoint, it seems clear that McCarthy's life was profoundly tragic. His native intelligence and formidable energy were largely squandered. He brought far more pain into the world than any man should. He was above all a reckless adventurer, an improviser, a bluffer. He once told a close friend, 'Remember, Gerry, he who does not live dangerously does not live at all.'"

Joe was no philosopher, and I question the validity of such a comment on his life. It doesn't sound like him at all. I was reporting in Cuba when he died and in Havana I sought out an editor with much experience in the observation of communist tactics.

"Nobody," she said, "could approve of the way Joe went about his work. But now that it's over, I wonder if there ever was any other way."

15.

The Losing Streak Begins

His hands were creased and shaky, he was turning gray at the eyebrows, he snapped hornrimmed glasses off and on over his eyes, into his pocket, all the while we talked in the Oval Office.

My last impression of President Kennedy was that the job had aged him far beyond its Thousand Days. He said that Bobby had told him I was taking a reporting trip to Latin America. "I thought you'd like to be briefed. Tell me what countries you'll be hitting."

I told him Venezuela, Brazil, Argentina and home via the Dominican Republic or Panama. He said, "By all means, Panama. Bobby's got a police training school there." JFK spoke in arithmetic about Latino economics and birth rates, and told me to visit his ambassadors. We were old friends, from his House and Senate days and his presidential campaign.

"Send your columns straight into here, so I won't miss any. When you're back, I want you to come again and brief me."

We laughed and he shoulder-slapped me as I left, saying, "Happy landings, amigo. That's a lot of flying."

My last impression of this grand, lovable guy was that he'd reached the White House about ten years before his time. He saw no anomaly in a liberal statesman's sponsoring a police school for storm troopers, as I discovered the Panama camp to be. With coaching and instruments from the Los Angeles police force, Latino graduates were learning how to keep existing Latin American governments in place by quelling resistance. The opposite purpose was shown in Kennedy's intervention to remove

Castro in Cuba. I felt in that last interview that the young President could recite statistics—birthrates and educational numbers for instance—without much comprehension of inner truths about peoples.

In fairness, which presidents of our postwar age have been up to the grave and grueling job? Truman, yes; Eisenhower, yes. JFK would begin the sorry line of one-term failures. It resembled the roll of chief magistrates between Andrew Jackson and Lincoln. The admired democracy, facing the crisis of emancipation and disunion, would do no better than Van Buren, W. H. Harrison, Tyler, Polk, Taylor, Pierce, Buchanan. And after Lincoln we had Andrew Johnson, U. S. Grant, R. B. Hayes, J. A. Garfield, Chester Arthur, Benjamin Harrison, William McKinley. Only Grover Cleveland, with a divided term, was worthy of reelection. Historians have tried unconvincingly to explain the dismal streak of bunglers. Another ran on after Kennedy through Johnson, Nixon, Ford and Carter. Perhaps we exaggerate the utility of a single leadership, and should find that the country's true strength is elsewhere—in its legislatures, courts, enterprise, productivity and inventiveness.

I went to Latin America and JFK went to Texas. No one forgets 11/22/63. I was crouching over a typewriter, deep in an extracurricular article for extra pay, when the door opened at 1931 National Press Building, and Mary hurried in from an early lunch. She broke the news with the succinctness of a wire service reporter:

"Jack Kennedy's been assassinated in Dallas, and Governor Connally is wounded."

I kept writing hard, not daring to break concentration on this piece. It was a half-hour before I went into the Press Club and asked the first member I encountered: "Is it true?"

He shouted, "Now look what you damned rightwingers have done!"

I asked the next man. "Yes, but damned if I'm going to cry when a politician goes out and gets shot while he's cadging votes."

These were the first reactions. There would be manly and feminine tears shed in profusion as the Capitol joined the ceremonies of parade, lying in state, services at the Cathedral and the Arlington gravesite.

My writings had supported Lyndon Johnson for the Democratic nomination, and Richard Nixon for the national election. I had traveled with all three. Personal attraction had nothing to do with it. Johnson was the peerless Majority Leader; Nixon the Eisenhower heir; Kennedy the charming young climber, an absentee in House and Senate. His eloquent Inaugural Address was the only warmth that reached the frigid press bleachers. His first 100 days gave us the disgraceful Bay of Pigs fiasco. No excuse would do. He had perpetuated a reckless, unprovoked, sneak attack on a small neighbor. He had lost his nerve to follow through. From then on nothing went right for America. Jack was our precursor of doom.

Yes, let us mark the calendar for that kickoff of disaster, Act One of calamity. The Democrats at Los Angeles might have done better in '60 to nominate Henry Jackson (he asked me to write a column for him in the *Los Angeles Times*). Or Stuart Symington ("My god," he told me, "I *did* want to be president!"). So did Adlai Stevenson, who once had quoted Christ and publicly asked that "this cup" be withheld, but now thirsted to quaff it. When JFK seemed to have got what he came to get, I asked, after midnight in Bob Kennedy's suite, about Jackson for vice-president. But he told me that his brother preferred Symington for a running mate. I asked Lyndon if he'd accept second place, and he blasted me, "As Majority Leader, I vote several hundred times in the Senate, would I change for a job where I might vote once a year?"

Johnson had convinced himself that he would stampede the convention. He knew the Senate, knew the Southern governors, he thought Carmine diSapio ran Tammany and could deliver. But Johnson knew little about the American people and less of foreign policy. Four years before, in 1956, while visiting him in Austin, I had urged him to go all out to become Stevenson's running mate. "Nobody's going to beat Ike," I said, "but just campaigning around the country will get you to know and be known." Lyndon snorted. He thought himself a household word because of his Senate leadership. In 1960 he barnstormed over the weekends, but did not run in the primaries, while Kennedy carried them all.

Campaign manager Bob Kennedy was less worried about the Catholic issue than the distrust by people of his father's millions and their influence. "Do you think we bought the West Virginia primary?" he asked me one night, a plaintive question, which convinced me that they had. I told him he had no worries, Jack would win, for no better reason than that it felt like a Democratic year.

Eisenhower's terms, while good for the country, had done nothing to strengthen the GOP.

Nixon had weakened the party. People remembered his blubbering Checkers speech, and his being spat upon in Venezuela. Stassen in '56 tried to bump Nixon from the ticket; Herter wanted to and would have grabbed a place on the Republican slate. President Eisenhower feared to drop his Vice-President; he'd been warned that the Republican rightwing would defect, as I felt sure it would.

Already in 1960 the conservative tide was rising; it wouldn't crest for another four years, but it was strong enough to force an eyelash race of Kennedy-Nixon. JFK almost certainly won on stolen votes in Texas and Chicago, and on the coattails of Lyndon and Lady Bird Johnson in the Old Confederacy.

After the Bay of Pigs defeat—but not before it—Kennedy apologists blamed the planning on Eisenhower, saying that preparation had gone too far to recede. But only the sitting president is the commander; battles are his to win or lose. It seems unlikely that Ike, with all his practice at seaborne invasions would have created the snafu, or allowed Nixon to do so.

JFK was at once too sportsmanlike to alibi his blunders and too artificial a hero to win against the toughies of the world—Khrushchev, Castro and Ho Chi Minh. His fall gave off a hollow sound which all the biographical dirges by his flunkies would not muffle.

It is probable that JKF's death spared this republic a Kennedy dynasty funded by dollars that bought the services of incense-throwers and subservient politicians. It is certain from the record that the Kennedy administration was a zero in domestic legislation and a loser of American prestige in Europe, Latin America, Asia and Black Africa.

Although I mourned Jack, I thought Johnson as president would be the peerless leader I'd seen on Capitol Hill. I wrote him a letter, wishing his administration well, and expressing gratitude that my children and grandchildren would have (as I thought) ten years of can-do government. LBJ immediately put through the Kennedy civil rights program, which required no more than a determined push. Otherwise, Johnson proved another hollow man. He marched 600,000 troops up the hill at Vietnam and marched them down again. He invoked no confidence at all from the American people. He bullied and lied to his subordinates and colleagues until the bankroll of good will that goes at first to every president was squandered in ill-spent blood and money.

LBJ was my friend and I would not have spoken or written this while he lived; a puzzling friendship, some said. I never supported his patched-up New Deal, nor his non-performance in Vietnam. Barry Goldwater often told me he could whip Kennedy, but that he had had no chance against Kennedy's empty cloak when wrapped around Johnson. Both 1964 conventions mirrored their parties' seething animosities. At San Francisco, the Republicans at last had an imperfect replica of Robert Taft. Not that Goldwater approached Taft in education, experience and family background, but Barry had the old-fashioned religion for honest enterprise. He abhorred the hokum and chummy posturizing of Nelson Rockefeller ("Hi-ya, fellah") and other me-too Republicans who had learned nothing from the defeats of Willkie and Dewey. Barry wasn't going to win any national election, but he refused to run for the White House "in tennis sneakers." He shook the GOP convention—and shocked the country—by coming out for extremism in pursuit of the noble goals.

As a president, Goldwater would have redirected Franklin Roosevelt's boast that "they" have met first "their match" and then "their master." FDR was vilifying citizens who had made an economic success in life while patronizing the underclasses; Goldwater wished to become the match-and-master of laborites, socialists and racial panderers. He set accomplishment above dependency in all cases.

Like Roosevelt, Kennedy, Rockefeller and Stevenson, Goldwater came from inherited wealth. He did not feel that he had to prove himself by taking the condescending line of false liberalism. I was not impressed with the outcries against Goldwater's extremism. On his campaign plane on Friday afternoon in New Mexico, we read the liberal innuendos that Barry had been "insane" since youth.

"Barry," I said, "if I had an interview with your family doctor, I might be able to spike that story."

He made a long distance call to Arizona and made an appointment with the family physician. The doctor took me to his office that Sunday in deserted downtown Phoenix. I crammed on Goldwater family medical records. Had it been barren of any nervous diagnosis, it would have lacked credibility. There was one, only one, doctor's notation that he had seen the privileged youth who'd become "overworked" in the uncongenial atmosphere of Goldwater's department store. Barry went back to flying, hiking and exploring Indian country—and was quite himself again. I rejoined the Republican campaigner, did two columns on my findings in Phoenix. They steel-hooped a friendship with Goldwater that was already set in concrete.

At Atlantic City in '64 the Democrats staged their special kind of melee over the secondary nomination behind President Johnson. LBJ practiced sadism from the catbird seat. When Bob Kennedy tried to stampede the delegates for himself by filming a tear-jerk movie on his brother, Lyndon outfoxed him by rescheduling the show until the nomination was final. The President used Senator Tom Dodd to bait Hubert Horatio Humphrey, whose ambition was as big as his heart. HHH didn't make the ticket without bootlicking the Texas tantalizer. All the while, Black Democrats on the boardwalks were howling their generations of hatred at the pale-faced Southerners who still ran the Democratic party. I came late to the farce and left early.

Unpredictably, Johnson, freed by his own election from the Kennedy martyrdom, showed us the weakest commander in chief since Buchanan and the most despised White House resi-

dent since Hoover. Lyndon's incumbancy brought us the shame
of drugged-up Yanks getting whipped by pigmy Orientals in
Vietnam. It featured the running dogs of anti-Americans in the
streets. He never could call the country to order. I was oftener in
the Oval Office than ever before or since, for LBJ groped everywhere for ideas, and implemented none. He'd lost the name of
action.

On the Thursday before the Sunday of his withdrawal from
competition, I came as close as I ever did to scooping a national
story.

Sam Houston Johnson, the scapegrace but wily brother who
for years had called Lyndon's political signals, phoned me at my
National Press Building office. Sam was sending an official car
which brought me to the Mansion's south entrance and to a rear
elevator.

In his third floor cubicle, Sam Houston circled the president/
subject. Down the hallway came young Luci Johnson Nugent,
holding her new baby. She thrust the child into my arms and
said, "His name's Lyndon, he's going to be President, too."

Were Sam and Luci telling me something? Elsewhere in the
mansion the Sunday address was being composed, but I did not
divine its message: the President would not seek nor accept
renomination.

Two years later, lonely and hurt in Texas exile, Lyndon Johnson went down in fatal heart attack. I did not attend the huge
funeral to which his body was brought from Austin to Washington and taken back to the family graveyard.

Instead of mingling with the celebrity hounds and the hypo-
critical haters who filled the National City Christian Church and
surrounding streets, I went alone to the chapel of my own
church and prayed for his unquiet soul.

While kneeling I treated my memory to the myriad of good
times—many more than this book would hold—that I had
shared with this indefinable personality.

16.

Faster Down the Chute

WHEN RICHARD NIXON, EX-PRESIDENT, lay sick and disgraced in his California home, he wrote "Dear Holmes and Mary" to say it was a time to know real friends and to send his thanks. The letter, unsolicited and unexpected, was made fuller in pathos by the wiggley signature of his full name that staggered across the width of the page.

There was more duration than proximity in my relationship with RN, as he customarily signed personal letters. He came to Washington, as I did, with the 80th Congress, our paths crossed often and the Nixons had us as guests in their private and public homes. It is a cliche that his shy and sinister nature shut him off from being "understood" as a human being, yet I found this to be true. My guess is that apart from his admirably loyal family, Nixon's best biographers would be his secretary, Rose Mary Woods, and his intimate, William Rogers, perhaps the only confidants in his public life.

My own feelings towards RN were a mix of fealty and chagrin. A major figure of our age, five times a national candidate, reelected president by forty-nine states, his opportunity to do good and govern well was as manifest as his sickening failure. "For God's sake, let us sit upon the ground and tell sad stories of the death of kings."

No tale is sadder than that of his wife, the more so because of its quiet monotony. In October 1952, the Republican candidate for vice-president made his final campaign stop at the Timonium Fair Grounds, near Baltimore. While Nixon and a gaggle of local candidates circled the race track in jeeps, gesticulating and gibbering in the tribal manner, I saw Pat Nixon sitting alone in the gazebo where winning jockeys weighed out. I introduced myself and opened with the hackneyed query, "How did you enjoy the crosscountry trip?" She burst out, "Oh, I think of nothing except to get home in Washington and to my babies."

In the many meetings ahead between us, I think she never varied from that theme. I'm sure she never discussed politics. Her life was not Dick; it was Tricia and Julie. On the 1960 whistle-stop train she came and sat beside me in the club car. She abruptly declared she felt torn from home and from her real duty to confiscate each morning's *Washington Post* with Herblock's carnivorous cartoons of Julie's and Tricia's dad, and to comfort them from the teasing of schoolmates. During 1968, in a limousine taking us to National Airport, I broke off questioning the GOP's presidential candidate to congratulate her on Julie's engagement to David Eisenhower. Pat Nixon's face glowed with a joy that had nothing to do with the possibility of victory over George McGovern.

I never analyzed the congeniality I felt with her, nor learned if she shared it. At one of the Sunday church services in the Nixon White House, she stood apart from her husband and bodyguards. I was turning elderly by then, was no doubt feeling patriarchal. She looked so forlorn that nothing seemed more fitting than to embrace and kiss (which, however, I didn't dare) an old friend with so much sorrow in her face.

"Oh," she said taking both my hands, "it's a good day when you can come here."

It was an unspoken empathy, though I never so much as used her first name as she did mine. While I write this, Mrs. Nixon has had a stroke, which is all too understandable, and is a route to understanding her difficult husband. On another White House occasion, an evening reception, I was in the Blue Room with the President and taking a champagne glass from a passing tray. He said without preface, "You know, to be a good football player, you've got to be very fast or very big, and I wasn't either."

Another cliche, I know, is that Dick Nixon's inferiority complex went back at least as far as his Whittier College days. Yet the remark was not something you expect to hear from a twice-elected vice-president and president. It says much about him and just as much about the American state of governance. By the 1970s, its disintegration was self-evident and alarming, after less than 200 years under the Constitution of 1787. Hamilton, among others of the Founders, thought of democracy as a wasting disease. It had crept into what was a republican compact. Up until the administrations of George Washington, the Virginia Dynasty and the Adamses, there was nothing that approached popular suffrage and government. Afterward, it seemed like blind luck when we chose a Chief Executive who approximated our estimation of the sacred grandeur of the office.

Nixon's unsinkable ambition, his pitiful unlovableness, his numerous misadventures, would appear in logic to have ruled him out of the presidency, most especially under the stormclouds of an on-going war and the acknowledged threat of a better-armed and self-declared enemy.

Why didn't the country produce someone to stop Nixon and his kind? We know that the 1876 election of Hayes was rigged by Federal bayonets, and that Kennedy's of 1960 was clouded. Nixon's attorney at the time, Bob Finch of California, told me he was retained to search the state statutes for some way to challenge the prima facie vote-stealing in Cook county, Illinois, and Duval county, Texas.

Had such laws existed, Nixon might well have overthrown Kennedy. JFK never felt he had a mandate in that narrow decision ("Nelson Rockefeller would have beaten me," he often said). Hubert Humphrey nearly stopped Nixon in '68, but the Johnson war-making shadow was said to be fatal.

We should ask—why so? HHH was a peacemonger if that's what the country wanted. The majority party of Democrats and the sober-thinking of a free people had every chance to eject Nixon, who repeatedly exhibited his unfitness.

I voted against Humphrey whom I knew and liked very well. But he was a World War II draftdodger, a pacifist at heart, a socialist in practice. The country at large seemed to find less fault than I did with these traits in HHH, but the rebellious Democrats shelved him.

In 1972 Nixon's win was made certain by an acme of ineptitude in George McGovern whose chief backers were Ban the Bomb unilateral disarmament buffs.

I have thought that the self-destruct compulsion which ran through Nixon's career and ultimately brought him down had become rooted in the American nation. The suicide drive, whether by transferrence or a natural growth, was evident in many ways. Not unnaturally, I thought back to my little-read book with its subtitle, *A Study in the Will to Win.* It is George Washington, the winner against all odds, not Robert E. Lee, the gentlemanly loser, who must become the subconscious mover and shaker for an on-going American nation.

Deep under Nixon's awareness of his inferiority, collaterally related to his yearning for statesmanship, lay a rockbed of professionalism. I think this explained my fealty to him. It fell short of real friendship and fondness which his elusive personality forbade. But the man had a deep-down ruthlessness, which is the property of leadership in Washington, Andrew Jackson, the Roosevelts, Truman and Churchill, the Anglo-American. In Nixon this trait broke ground with his Christmastime '72 mining of Haiphong and the bombing of Hanoi.

For just that short period, in defiance of popular protest, Nixon became the man he always wanted to be. He stood as the man I could admire. His limited purpose of retrieving the POWs was accomplished, but too late to win the war, too late to stop the domino-falling of Southeast Asia to Asian communism.

This smidgeon of heroism in Nixon, of course, was no offset to his failings. A leader of gigantic force was needed to squelch our atomic guilt, overcome the loser complex, arouse the population which in the 18th, 19th and early 20th century had produced all-conquering soldiery. Only in that flash of killer-instinct did Nixon stand up and play the man.

Watching his national career all the way, I saw what every covering newsperson saw—that basically Nixon was unpresidential and superficial. Although he schemed against Knowland and Warren to be Eisenhower's running mate, he was surprised when the Knight papers announced the ticket. I asked publisher Jack Knight about the episode; he archly replied, "Well, we don't tell Dick everything."

Losing to Kennedy and essaying a comeback in 1962 via the California governorship, Nixon straddled the two controversial issues, the anti-labor right-to-work matter and endorsement by the John Birch Society. That year in Los Angeles, I remonstrated with him over the first. He interrupted to say, "You don't understand; in this state it's impossible to win against the labor vote." He repudiated the Birchites.

In both instances, he was going hard against his personal beliefs. His primary opponent, Assemblyman Joe Shell, boldly told me he was anti-labor and a Birchite. Shell took one-third of the Republican primary vote and caused Nixon's defeat in the general election. Four years later, I was covering Reagan's first run for the governorship. RR was no Birchite, but he did not strike the holy pose of repudiation.

"I figure that if the Birchites vote for me, they're endorsing my program—I'm not endorsing theirs."

Reagan's forthrightness won the governorship as Nixon's evasiveness had lost it.

When Nixon found himself in the Eisenhower administration, he took up golf at middle-age, and urged me to do the same, as if it were a patriotic duty in support of Ike. He showed me his library, proud of the condensed volumes of great works and of collections of quotable quotes. Nothing about him was vicious, only sophomoric in a sweating effort to please, to conform and meanly to succeed. Today people will ask about Watergate—"But what did he *do*?"—questioning whether the punishment of being driven from office was too harsh. I think this question of over-punishment will be around long after Nixon and his generation are gone. We consider it uncivilized when Muslim adultresses are publicly stoned to death and thieves are lawfully maimed. So with Richard Nixon who was grossly over-punished. Superficial, sophomoric, unworthy of his office he clearly was, but I doubt if the country will always feel satisfaction in dishonoring this feckless creature.

The whole matter belongs in the deep perspective of our times. Everything that can be said against Nixon is a sad indictment of America. Was he friendless? So was America throughout the world. Was he a wastrel of great opportunities? Was he ignorant of great matters that were sweeping the world? Was he capable of meanness and cruel trickeries? All the questions can be asked—and regrettably answered—about the U.S.A of Nixon's era, to say nothing of Kennedy's and Johnson's.

Perhaps it is the worst of times and perhaps RN was the worst of presidents. But these are hard judgments, and the future is its customarily opaque self. As an onlooker, I shun any appearance of presumptuousness, not being in Nixon's confidence nor in public service. But since action is always preferable to its absence, I wish that Nixon had joined the contest of impeachment and trial instead of running away. It is far from certain that the bills, drawn by the House Judiciary committee and assured of ratification by the House itself, would have withstood a determined fight in the Senate. In any event, it would have become a national leader to go down fighting. Barbara Tuchman has written that it also became Congress to rely on the Constitution which provides for the removal of a president for "high crimes or misdemeanor." Both the President and the Congress were out of line to opt for resignation.

Again, the parallel of Nixon and his country is real and startling. That we have become weakened from neglect and apathy, that we have lost the support of our allies, that our chances in a pitched battle against World Communism do not seem rosy is all lamentably true. But the only everlasting truth we know of is that nothing is impossible to stouthearted leadership—that thither lies our quest.

How blunderingly our self-government failed us in Nixon's immediate successors. The mishmash of the 25th Amendment allowed the selective elevation of Gerald Ford from minority floor leader to the post of a non-elected president. It placed him where he could and did pardon Nixon, at the time an "unindicted co-conspirator." It permitted Ford to name the oft-rejected Nelson Rockefeller as vice-president, one heartbeat away from a post where neither the party or the country wanted him.

Altogether, the American system proved ludicrously unable to recover from its plunge into the netherlands of existence. Loss of our first war, our first dismissal of a president by non-constitutional process and the world televised bathos of a farewell that would have shamed a loin-cloth or banana republic did nothing to inspire us to recovery of self-respect.

Many like myself had hoped and expected that Gerald Ford would live up to his reputation of unadorned honesty and play the selfless patriot. He would, I thought, make an honest woman of the repeatedly betrayed Republic by leading her as soon as possible to a lawful head of household. Ford would do this by serving out the Nixon term and retiring unsullied and undefeated to Grand Rapids—no doubt to an ovation worthy of any hero who'd ridden through a ticker tape parade. President Ford hit the front pages with a wide smile and an outstretched hand to welcome George Meany to the Oval Office, a gesture of brotherhood and good feeling which promised that sort of refreshing regime.

But as Jack Kennedy had jocularly remarked, there was a captivating swing to the tune "Hail to the Chief," and evidently it gave Gerry Ford the tickle-toe. I attended his first press conference, another symbolic scene. Instead of standing against the backdrop of the blank wall of the East Room as his predecessors had, Ford stood before an open door through which we could see into the Executive household—an everyman's home for a weary and much-deceived people to observe that this genuine man had nothing in his life or heart to conceal.

Shortly afterwards, with a half-dozen columnists, I attended a White House breakfast in the Roosevelt Room. TR's portrait now hung there and would remain until FDR's likeness in the same place indicated a Democratic takeover. President Ford, at the head of an oblong table, was relaxed and jovial, and he was borrowing lines from the country's most colorful Republican, Ronald Reagan, who for a decade or more had been preaching the removal of big government from the peoples' backs. Sure enough—Mr. Ford pitched into the Pentagon which he vowed to slim down. I believed, as did Reagan and most of other Americans, that waste though there be, the Defense Department was the only one with any excuse for being hefty. I asked a question with that implication and the president said huffily, "No department will be immune, Holmes."

I recall walking back to the National Press Building with

Roscoe Drummond and thinking that Gerry Ford was question-quibbling like a candidate finding his stride. I remembered some years back the meeting in the House of Representatives when Gerald Ford had benefited in a deal where he became House minority floor leader over Melvin Laird, perhaps the brightest man in politics. Had the deal gone otherwise, Laird might be acting president. No Washington correspondent would be likely to deny that he had a more presidential intellect than Ford. Only in his forthright recapture of the merchant ship *Mayaguez* did Gerald Ford make his country look like a major power, in heart-throbbing contrast to the way his successor would allow the fifty-two hostages to fester in Iranian prisons. For the rest, he seemed a kindly, lackluster dullard at a time when the nation was famishing for the post-Nixon greatness that certainly must be lurking somewhere in a country which so many could remember as the wonder of the world.

What the Republican Convention of '76 at Kansas City showed us was the imperialistic undertow of the incumbancy to nominate its successor. "That poor, pathetic mudturtle, Lord Hoover" (Mencken's phrase) kept the depression-cursed nomination in '32; the greenhorn Truman not only chose himself in '48 but dragooned Adlai Stevenson in '52. So it was with President Ford, battered bridegroom of an unconsumated honeymoon; he left Ronald Reagan knocking on the fast-closed door. And Jimmy Carter, from a party still demoralized by Johnson, Humphrey and McGovern, got away with offering the United States a well-meaning sad sack vagabond from Georgia.

Once, when an incumbant president and vice-president happened to be abroad, I wrote a facetious column to the point that we didn't need these figureheads, anyhow; that the country, like a well-ordered household, could run itself surprisingly well. I was spoofing, of course, but President Jimmy Carter's incumbancy made the jest sound like the true word. Carter's pretentious habit of carrying his own luggage aboard planes, his showoff walk with Rosalynn along Pennsylvania Avenue on Inauguration Day, his *Playboy* magazine revelation that he often "sinned" by looking at women with lust, his self-proclaimed born-again Christianity, his revolting speech in Mexico in which he

referred to his bout with Montezuma's Revenge were occasions
when the country might well have wished that nobody was presi-
dent. Often it became a case of ABC (Anybody But Carter).
What kind of Chief Executive would permit UN Ambassador
Andy Young to barge in on foreign policy so arrogantly that Mr.
Carter had to fire him or lose his Secretary of State, Cyrus
Vance? Was it true Christianity to send a man in the terminal
stages of cancer, the former Shah of Iran, an American ally, to
find a foreign bed in which to die? For a while we thought
President Carter had presided over a peace-forever Camp David
Accord—until the pact began to show Mideast daylight through
its loopholes. The unbelievable imprisonment of diplomats and
Marines in Tehran and the fatal botch of the Desert One rescue
mission seemed a tragic Keystone Kops scenario.

Jimmy Carter's unseating of the shaky Gerald Ford threw
honest doubt on the efficacy of "consent of the governed." Carter's posturing as the Uriah Heep of human rights not only
discredited our capacity for self-government, but raised the
spectre of a caretaking tyranny at home.

Fortunately, although President Carter in his own vulgar lingo
"whipped the ass" of Ted Kennedy and commandeered his own
renomination, he was unable to engineer his election. Ronald
Reagan, determined that there would be at least forty presidents,
hit his stride in the spring of 1980, breezed through sufficient
primaries, conducted a silent prayer at the Republican Convention in Detroit, and out-communicated Carter in their one-on-
one debate.

If America had historically sinned, as none could deny, if our
own trespasses were those of omission to sanitize our industries
and cleanse our politics and reform our welfare, we had been
brought to the time of atonement. Murphy's Law—everything
that could go wrong seemingly had done so—prevailed.

Eligible voters became non-voters in increasing numbers,
which could be called a non-aggressive protest. The stage-man-
aged party system, susceptible to corruption and gun-shy of the
home truths, had absurdly flopped. No programs from Kennedy
through Carter were activated—though many were verbalized—
to revitalize our dying industries. Our arrogant labor leaders

were housed in marble palaces and often dominated by gangsters. Our mendicants in increasing number demanded and got
bread, subsidies and education from the bankrupt Federalia.
Our suffocating immigration tidal wave seemed the aftermath of
the involuntary immigration by African slavery. The central
matter of national defense had become an ugly medley of mu-
tiny, dope addiction, homosexual permissiveness and cowardice.

As we broke into the 1980s, Ronald Reagan looked to be the
last chance. Prediction is not a human potential—we just never
know! If history is an honest guide, Reagan had better succeed
lest fascism or foreign domination lies around the next turn.

17.

The Steepening Decline

"HONEY, NEVER SPEND A TWO-CENT STAMP TO MAKE AN ENEMY," was the advice passed on to Mary by her father, a wholesale shoe manufacturer, and relayed to me, a retailer of words.

Long after the golden years of the two-cent stamp, she applied the aphorism to fan mail and editorial comment. In the years of commuting from Baltimore, I kept secretaries and dictated the mail, giving blow-for-blow. But as our children grew up Mary came to the office and brought her father's advice.

She did not lick stamps to make readers angry. She turned on the Dixie charm, not sickly sweet, but with an air I would have to call "fey." She captivated a letter-writer as lightly as toying with a glove. If a reader had praised a column, she praised his taste. If he damned it, she bade him wait for the next. In every instance, she would quote the writer's letter to show that she'd read it. She always urged him to write or call the editor in my behalf. She signed as "H.A."

It was subtle promotion, done with the grace of seeming carelessness. My secretaries were trained for professional perfection, and put out regimented correspondence. Mary's system was uneven, even helter-skelter, much more of an attention-getter than perfection. The thing proved itself, for soon she had a nationwide stable of pen pals who thought they were hearing from me. As the mail grew heavier, we invested in post cards with the printed message, "Thank you for writing," but the cards never went out without a scribble from her to give them personal warmth.

Ours was a no lose policy. We turned many a feudist into a friend, won the cold heart of many an editor who would be astonished to hear from a local reader in my behalf. ("I have more relatives than Gracie Allen," Mary would say.) She also had Hollins College classmates whom she recruited for the cause. And friends she had made at the teachers' college of Columbia and the University of Virginia, and old beaux.

She wrote unsolicited letters over her own name to celebrities. Barney Baruch and Herbert Hoover were urged to put in a good word for a columnist who was serving the Conservative Movement. Astounded by the naïve approach after being jaded with sleek favor-seeking, these elder statesmen, among others, succumbed to powers of suggestion. There were times when I thought she overdid it. Once she surreptitiously incorporated a salespitch into a note of condolence to the widow of a certain former president. It may have been the only instance when her postage stamp irked its recipient. I would remonstrate but she would proceed on course.

McNaught Syndicate discovered that its columnist's wife was both a southern belle and a super salesperson. I think this came about when she negotiated a side-benefit in my contract whereby the Syndicate paid the entire office rent (I had paid half to this point). Since I traveled to report local elections and newsworthy events (power dams, ship launchings and the like), the Syndicate did not object when I called on editors to engage their interest. McNaught found it profitable to pay my wife's expenses as well as my own.

She would take deadly aim at close quarters. I saw her lean across a desk in West Virginia and make a sale by saying to a recalcitrant publisher, "Sir, *why* don't you buy my husband's column?" Once we had a cancellation in Georgia, and she flew there alone, staying with friends, and in three minutes with the publisher had a re-sale. "Mary, what did you *do* in there?" gasped her hostess.

Then there was an eccentric lady in Florida, known as Edie Coo Coo, who had no journalistic interests, but was a social matriarch. Mary persuaded her to mention me to a susceptible publisher, and he bought my feature. When my biography of

Alexander Hamilton was riding the rejection circuit, she made a long distance call to an inaccessible book publisher who surrendered by sending me a contract with advance royalty.

Readers wrote in because my pieces had readability, and Mary had a hand in that also. If I seemed to have rapidly vaulted from courthouse reporter to magazine staff editor to syndicated columnist, it was under her unobtrusive coaching. Pomposity is the byliner's occupational hazard, and she inoculated me against it. "Make 'em laugh, make 'em feel, make 'em *think* that they're thinking," she would say.

Mixed with hard-news interviews and heady philosophizing on the downfall of the nation, I threw in a change-of-pace with satire and buffoonery. When Henry Wallace was a presidential candidate in '48, I wrote straight-faced pleas to state governors that they invoke the insanity statutes and lock up Henry as a public fool and menace. The proof I offered was that the itinerant candidate often lost track of his schedule. He would ad lib to the good people of South Carolina when he was in North Carolina. He would laud West Virginians while in the Old Dominion, mistake his Wilmingtons, Salems and Albanys.

These are commonplace goofs in political campaigns, but I thought the pinko Wallace was a goofy character, a Soviet stooge, and the spoofing came off well. Recalling how Quisling gave his name to the language, I nonsensically applied the idea to the Progressive Party runner. My columns said:

"How dare you wallace with my daughter's affections . . . he was confined to a wallace asylum . . . persons of that name are too embarrassed to sign it on hotel registers . . . it's disappeared from hundreds of telephone directories for the same reason."

Such efforts brought mail tumbling into the office. I experimented further. My column for the day after Truman upset Dewey in '48 (as Mary had predicted at the GOP convention) had this lead: "Pass the crow, darling. Also another gallon of hemlock tea. . . ."

At her suggestion, I called up invented characters and pretended to interview them: "Whatever happened to the United States of America?" asked the Returning Traveler who'd been away for a while. "Was the country overrun and ravished by the Visogoths?"

No, the despot's heel was never on our shore, the Traveler was sternly told. But America has been busy at self-destruction. You see. . . .

Another character was Dr. Clarence W. Couchmaster, master of the psychiatric couch.

"You say you keep seeing a man with a beard?" asked Dr. Couchmaster gently of the handsome young man on his couch. "And he won't go away?"

"If I hadn't chickened out at the Bay of Pigs," answered the jittery patient, "the bearded devil wouldn't sit every night at my bedside. All I had to do was show more courage and less profile, but. . . ."

Dr. Couchmaster "interviewed" Eisenhower, Stevenson, Acheson, the great and near great of the day. There were other invented persons; some of the newspapers ran the column with sketched illustrations of Dr. Couchmaster, the Returning Traveler and Horace W. Hollerguy "who always hollered like that." Some editors indignantly refused to use these "talking animals." Readers wrote to say they couldn't find my master psychiatrist in *Who's Who* or the medical directories.

I used this fictive method sparingly. I wasn't a humorist to match Art Buchwald, the late Fred Othman, the late George Dixon and other funny fellows. I didn't challenge them. My stock in trade was forthright conservatism. I was for protective tariffs and against forced race-mixing; for Barry Goldwater and against Walter Reuther; I was against entangling alliances and for America right or wrong.

These positions drew fervid responses, but I was never a "knee-jerk" rightwinger. Hate mail abounded when I seemed to switch ideologies. Early on, I asserted the right of Larry Parks to "sing" the Al Jolson Story. I had a "summer romance" when I preferred Jack Kennedy over Dick Nixon in the hot months of '60, though I later came out for Nixon in November. I made a hero of the magnificent ex-socialist, Senator Paul Douglas. I always liked personable Democrats such as the Kennedy brothers, the Johnson brothers, Bill Fulbright, Bill Proxmire, Mike

Mansfield, Stuart Symington. I puzzled many readers, infuriated others, delighted Hubert Humphrey when I picked him as the All Star Senator of a session. I enjoyed stirring up the wolves.

What I didn't notice, until a critic pointed it out, was that I was changing from what he called "a private man to a public man." This can happen without fame or fanfare, as was true with me. Mary was aware of the transition when I was not, as we drew progressively closer.

In retrospect, the occasion that took me out of the closet occurred in the early '50s when the late Senator Harry Byrd began inviting us to his annual Sunday dinners at his Berryville estate. Only the elite made his guest list—his neighbors, the President and Vice-President, his favored fellow-Senators, his chosen few among writers. To be in the Byrdhouse was to have "arrived."

Two special gestures of his put me on Byrd's Honors List. One was when he kissed Mary goodbye as we left his home. The other was, when he knew he was dying, he dictated a dandy introduction to my book, *Washington and Lee*. Since Jack Kennedy did the introduction of another book, *The Famous Five*, I had endorsement from the respectable Right and the respectable Left. As a syndicated columnist, I had gone public.

In the Eisenhower years, Khrushchev threatened to take over Berlin, and I rode over on a military plane. I'd asked my wife if she would like to go to Frankfurt, which she took to mean Kentucky, not West Germany. She had never been abroad, and was pleased when I booked her on a commercial flight. At the airport, in New York, her passport was rejected as faulty. She pluckily phoned the State Department (half deserted that day because of Secretary Dulles's funeral) and demanded special privilege. She was allowed to board by agreeing to meet me and submit to arrest at Frankfurt by the Military Police.

We applied for a new passport in that city, and went on to West Berlin and a Mayor Willy Brandt multilingual press conference. I knew I had an all-around partner when Mary caused the Mayor to turn his back on a dozen foreign reporters and discuss the European situation with her in English.

After that I repeatedly took her with me overseas. We went

together to Greece and Turkey, to Portugal and Spain, to England and France, to South Africa, the French Congo, Rhodesia, Cuba, Ulster, Venezuela, Chile, Peru, Argentina, Formosa and Japan. I left her behind when I went to trouble zones—Russia, Morocco, Korea, Vietnam and the warring Belgian Congo. She helped me size up American generals, admirals, ambassadors and Batista. In our four decades of marriage I made many judgmental errors about persons and business, but only when I wasn't taking her advice.

It was an era, from Jack Kennedy through Gerald Ford to Jimmy Carter, when America was sickening—and so, imperceptibly at first, was Mary. I was faster at discerning the country's ailments than my wife's, but I saw an analogy between her sinking and that of the sinking presidencies. There were many ominous signs. She did not eat and would not walk. Her mind was failing. Like a lovely tree she and the nation were dying from the top.

We tried all the "miracles": the psychiatrist's couch and electroshock treatments, university and private hospitals, a doctor-run clinic in a classy apartment house, a day-nurse who stood on her rights to do no housework, an expensive nursing home high above Wisconsin Avenue, our Episcopal church retreat where costs were just as high but the humaneness was much better.

At no time could a physician give her ailment a name. Some years later I saw a newspaper piece on "Alzheimer's disease" (premature senility) and a doctor identified it and admitted that this was the insoluble problem.

There were periods of remission when the patient was better rather than worse and could be at home with maid service. We were told nothing was wrong that "rest" would not mend. She wasn't enthusiastic about my suggestion of a luxury cruise on the Queen Elizabeth to England, with a ten-day stop-off at Cambridge where I had attended Trinity College and written my first book. "Just the thing," said our society-shrink. "Make her go if you have to sedate her."

We went by wheelchair to Union Station and in New York by the same means to dockside and stateroom. On a previous trip to Cambridge, she had shared my nostalgia—not this time. We wheelchaired and train-rode to the 1976 Republican Convention in Kansas City, the Democratic Convention in New York. St. Elizabeth's, the federal mental hospital, was suggested. It was free and probably the best in the country, but I balked at a public institution.

Self-pity, the lowest form of human emotion, I never indulged in. She was the sick person; I was not. But one morning in the Dirksen Senate Office Building, while exchanging ideas with columnist Paul Scott, my knees buckled and I hit the floor. I was instantly up, but Scott took me to the Senate infirmary where the nurse said, "Get him to a hospital." Scott and a taxi driver hurried me to the emergency entrance of George Washington Hospital, and a cardiac team took over. "Don't worry," its captain said, "we just saved Judge Sirica. You'll make it."

Several hours later, I was dismissed with instructions to go home in a cab and go to bed. But Mary was several miles distant at the Sibley Hospital mental clinic, and I swallowed two stiff drinks and taxied there for the daily visit.

These were lonely days. Aside from Scott, I don't think anybody in the press corps peeped a word of sympathy. My wife had friends who faithfully called, as did the clergy of the Church of the Epiphany, and our children rallied. I had to keep writing, five days a week by contract.

Whatever had happened to the United States of America, this sick man of an invalid world? We knew how ill the country was, but could not find the root causes. My God, the sickness ran on dual tracks for me. Whatever had happened to Mary?

"Mary has lost her mind."

Aghast, one night at a press reception I heard myself speak these horrifying words. A friend and colleague of many years, columnist Jack Kilpatrick, stood with me as we held highballs and talked inconsequentially, when out of politeness he asked me about my wife. I had never before used the language of my reply. Dime-store psychology tells us that we repress matters we find painful and private. Sometimes, as in this instance, they are buried so deep that we subconsciously deny their reality.

I had spoken impulsively, not measuring my words. Kilpatrick, a Richmond editor who had bought my column twenty-some years before turning columnist himself, sprang back when I spoke. He seemed stunned with shock. He could only make incredulous sympathetic sounds. I nodded in affirmation and moved into the throng.

My burst-out statement had hit me like a knife wound. Few experiences are so brutal as facing up to an unwelcome truth. Of course, I had never forgotten the forty-years-past disturbance that rocked our youthful marriage. Had I taken mature and professional counseling at that time, I would have treated her nervous breakdown and suicide attempt as incurable. The doctors, nurses and my father all counseled permanent confinement.

I refused. Instead, I signed the legal documents for responsibility. I didn't believe in miracles, but in college I'd read Ernest Renan's *Life of Jesus* in which the biographer dismisses the myth of divinity and explains Joshua (Jesus was a derivative) as a gentle person of extraordinary empathy. This trait had enabled Jesus to heal deranged spirits (especially in disturbed women), according to Renan. I felt my young wife could be healed by everyday human love and the benignity of Nature. We slept with our wrists tied together, and each day for three spring and summer months walked and drove in the bright blooming Maryland weather. She got well, and we thought it would be forever and ever.

By now, the Ford-Carter campaign of '76 was wasting, and I had seen little of it. With a small group of columnists I did have a White House breakfast interview with President Ford, but because of Mary I had to cancel a talk in Atlanta with Governor Carter. I tried to recoup the serious newsgathering gap with two contacts when Carter sped through Washington.

It was obvious that my column needed out-of-town travel and datelines, equally plain that I had an invalid wife. Perhaps I could make do with a fast trip. In Indianapolis, my friend Dick Lugar, former Mayor, was running for the Senate against the Democratic incumbant, Vance Hartke. It made a conservative v. liberal contest, my favorite kind.

"You'll be okay?" I asked Mary. "I'll go on a morning plane and be back by night."

"That'll only wake me up," she said. "Please stay overnight in Indianapolis. I'm going to dinner with Peggy Guggenheim. She's sending her car and will see me home."

Next day Dick Lugar's press secretary met my plane in Indianapolis. By late afternoon I had talked with him and had my story. In the airport hotel bedroom I heard the TV debate between the President and the Georgia Governor, and so had two subjects. On the morning flight into Washington I easily did the Lugar column. At home I found the daily paper on my doorstep and settled down to scan it, allowing my wife the luxury of a late sleep.

While I read, there came faint thumpings from above. I went up there with curiosity, without premonition. A nightgowned body had fallen between the twin bed and the wall. On the floor lay a vial of pills, some of them scattered over the bed. A police ambulance responded promptly to my call. I rode with the muttering patient to the George Washington Hospital emergency entrance. When my wife died almost a year later, the head of McNaught Syndicate wrote me, "Wherever she's gone, we're sure she's out there bragging about her Holmes."

18.

How It Ends

IN THE GREAT NOVELS—I think of *War and Peace, Vanity Fair*, the *Forsyte Saga*—all roads lead to home and end there. It takes gifted literary artistry to bring it off, and I don't expect that. But I wrote an article that made the attempt.

"One Happy Marriage Deserves Another," Holmes Alexander (from *Washington Post Magazine*, 1/28/79).

Life, I wrote, which is short enough and not always very sweet, belongs to the living, as death too often comes to remind us. A lady I loved long and devotedly, my wife since 1934, recently died at 73, and the heart of the article is that I remarried just fifteen days later.

Indecent haste? Callous self-indulgence? A lot of people probably thought so. "Dear sir. You may be right," was H. L. Mencken's standard repartee to abusive fan letters brought on by his free-swinging essays, columns, books and ad lib quips.

Mencken's response always was nonpareil. At my first wedding he wrote me: "I can only give you my blessing. My marriage, now in its fifth year, has been a whopping success—and I rattle my chains with loud hosannas."

So it was with Mary and me. Despite the anguish of one whose wife was periodically mad and suicidal, I had a loving, laughing marriage with her, as our friends all knew. But with her death I determined, at 72, not to deny myself whatever joie de vivre remained. I write this hortatory message to my contemporaries: take cheer and do likewise. One happy marriage deserves another.

Given half a chance, love will find a way. Medical writers long

147

ago demolished the theory that sex declines and disappears with
age, and every elderly couple will learn on their own that a new
partner brings stimulation and innovations. A common obstacle
to remarriage is the disapproval of grown children whose objec-
tions, often unspoken or insinuated, range from true respect for
the deceased parent to threatened loss of inheritance and a
wishful belief from ignorance that it's a case of all-passion-spent
for elderly newlyweds. But the golden age belongs only to those
who live it.

Overly anxious parents raised me to be shy and timid, but at
an early age I read Davy Crockett's motto: "Be sure you're right,
then go ahead." It impressed me indelibly. There would be scores
of occasions in war and peace, in sports, politics and journalism
when many persons thought my judgment atrocious, and spoke
and showed their disapproval. But I blundered ahead with no
better than indifferent success in life, though blessed with fun,
love and luck. If I keep my buttons, it will be that way to the end.
I recommend Davy's advice to those recently bereaved and hit
hard by natural sorrow.

Mary's people, though well-fixed with the usual number of
Virginia manor houses and attendants, were professional by nature. Her grandfather was a beloved circuit court judge for fifty
years. His portrait still hangs in half a dozen Southside court-
houses. Her favorite uncle, after winning a World War I Distinguished Service Cross for valor, spent most of his adult
manhood on state and federal benches. Another uncle was the
surgeon-in-chief at a large hospital. There had been money in
the family from the Craddock Terry Shoe factory at Lynchburg,
but business was drooping. There was talent on the maternal
side: one of her uncles won a Smithsonian award for building a
miniature steam engine. An aunt who studied with Mary Cassatt
was honored in her lifetime by the Georgia Morgan Art Gallery
in Lynchburg.

When we met and became engaged we both were school
teachers, jobs that were secure in the 1930s Depression. Better
men than I were released from positions in which they performed well—the business just wasn't there.

I was, at 26, being modestly published. So with financial advances from an indulgent father, I resigned my safe teaching job and forfeited a seat in the Maryland House of Delegates. I moved from the hunting shires of Maryland to a cheap hotel in Greenwich Village. Crockett would have told me, "Write or starve."

I had some luck with the magazines, and managed to marry after a year of Grub Street. Neither fame nor fortune came to me, but there was a ragtime of the day, "Ain't We Got Fun," and we did, with muted hosannas. At the end Mary was in and out of mental institutions for the better part of three years, a wife by then in name only, until a Georgetown University Hospital doctor gave it to me in an emergency phone call.

"I'm sorry, sir. Your wife has just passed."

I would feel selfish to omit the sequel. Mary and I heard of a group of golf-playing retirees in Florida who pledged that when a member died, his cronies would bear him to the cemetery and inter him, with as little of the law's delay as possible, in the clothes he was wearing. She and I, living in Foggy Bottom on the campus of George Washington University Medical School, learned of the school's body donation unit and obtained and exchanged contracts with the school to receive us both at death.

I will not pretend I was without emotional disturbance when I notified the University morgue, arranged for the transportation and took care not to view the remains. I soon was in receipt of a thoughtful letter from the donations director who thanked us both for a valuable contribution to science and gave assurance the body would be treated with the utmost respect.

For a while I found it difficult not to shudder when daily passing the mortuary building adjacent to the subway station by which I went to work. The imagination can be cruel. To those who may come to my experience, I can say that the human imagination is also subservient to its owner. I coached myself to understand the grim gray building, where I at last would go. It was not essentially different from the village cemetery.

Lindy, my second wife, 69, had been a girl of exquisite beauty, granddaughter of a Maryland governor and founder of the Fidelity Trust Company. I had known her since our Baltimore dancing class. I tell her today that we were childhood sweethearts, but she says that is fantasizing. To her I was part of a prep school corps which she royally regarded as being individually and collectively in love with her. The boy whose affection she decided to reciprocate was a school chum; and we were barely past college age when he asked me to be among his ushers. They made the handsomest couple of the season, and I was content to be no more than their close friend.

Hardly a year later Lindy's husband was my usher, and she traveled to Virginia for my ceremony where she glowed as gay a beauty as Scott Fitzgerald ever portrayed. To my credit I wasn't noticing. I had found the girl of my heart.

Lindy's marriage wobbled along for ten years. The match succumbed to one of those best-friend relationships with a man who had once openly vowed to have her for his wife. The second husband, a successful thoroughbred race horse trainer, was a tough one to beat, as I found him in the steeplechases. He was also a heavy drinker and tough to live with. So she divorced him. Lindy moved in with her mother. I paid a midnight visit where I pled the case for sticking out the first marriage, a useless and altruistic plea.

At that point I was firmly married with three children, books and magazine stories in print and soon to be off to World War II. Lindy went to Reno, returned to marry and to a picturesque farm in Howard County between Baltimore and Washington. Writing to them from the 2nd Bombardment Group (H) in the European Theater of Operations, I congratulated her on the arrival of a son and daughter, but she did not answer.

Ten years went by, ten years more, and it was not until 1976, while on a speaking engagement in Baltimore, that I was ever alone with Lindy, a platonic encounter where I practiced the delivery of my speech. Two more years passed, and with my unhappy wife in the Home for the Incurables, I ventured to ask Lindy for luncheon at the Belvedere Hotel in Baltimore. I wondered aloud why she hadn't remarried.

"Oh, there's nobody. You see, I'm a burned-out case."

"No, I don't believe it. I only wish I were in a position to prove otherwise."

I desperately wanted to bring Lindy into my life, but there

were taboos. I asked the assistant rector of my church if I could take her to a service as a guest.

"There would be talk," he said gently but firmly.

But we continued weekly luncheons as I traveled the Metroliner from Washington to Baltimore, and we pined like people fifty years younger.

At home in Washington I fell into the shambles of a loner's life, going regularly to see my wife, sleeping in a bed that was made only on days the part-time maid came.

As a journalist I had to rise early, but after Capitol Hill coverage and lunch at the Press Club, I filed my daily piece and went back to bed with a tumbler of whiskey which knocked me out for two hours. After that, feeding myself coffee and canned food, I worked long into the night on a book. My weight swelled by nearly forty pounds, and my column lost that many clients. I would drink again after midnight till I slept.

Then, quite suddenly it seemed to me, came the death call, and all was over.

My children and friends gathered at the church for a memorial service for which I had chosen the psalms and hymns that Mary had liked, and for the first time in the long ordeal I broke down.

But I had a redeemer who will never wear a halo. Davy Crockett got through to me. "Be sure you're right; then go ahead."

Many in my age group, as the obituary pages bear daily testimony, undergo this mortal separation, and I address them from the heart. Reconstruction of life for any survivor born near the beginning of the century should begin as soon as he can meet Davy's first requirement. For myself, I knew that Lindy was right for me. It only remained to get on with it.

First, I took my daughter, mother of five, from the church to the Foggy Bottom home where Lindy made us a meal. The two had not met since Madge was a child, but they were instantaneously compatible on the pertinent subject, which was myself. Lindy said she loved me, but nothing on earth would bring her to marry another drunk. Madge said, "I hope you'll marry my father, but I worked one summer in his office and I know he's not easy to please."

This was the jury I faced, and I pleaded nolo contendere. I didn't care for the water wagon but I promised a curfew on the midday and midnight drinking if only she would have me. I would take only "happy hour" cocktails with her. When that system didn't work, I quit cold turkey, and with some dieting the forty surplus pounds fell away.

The rest is all downhill. I visited the rector of my church, and asked instructions. He told me to go quite soon to the district courthouse for a civil marriage, and to serve the decent interval until the union could be sanctified in church.

So Lindy and I, after being properly licensed, stood up in the district court chambers of Judge Oliver Gasche, a classmate with whom I had recently celebrated our 50th Princeton reunion. We had only one attendant, a black man, Air Force Sergeant Carl Sensabaugh, who had begun as a handyman and ended as a friend during Mary's long illness.

He drove us to and from the courthouse, and afterward at home there was a surprise. The part-time maid, no less a friend after this, had brought out the long-unused linen, the often-unpolished silver. She treated us to a four-seated wedding luncheon.

Not many from my end of the century will be as lucky as this.

Addendum

A Veteran Columnist Lays Down His Pen

KEY WEST, FLA.—All of us who have lived stressfully need decompression, private or institutional, at the withdrawal period. Few had better company and more portentous surroundings than I did on January 20, 1981. There in "Working Press" under the Capitol's west wall, I listened to the Inaugural Address which declared a new freedom for America. Behind the instant President sat his weary discard, while in the same forgiving sky of a warm winter noontime the freed captives of Tehran were leaving Iranian airspace.

Big with emotion was this occasion for me. Amid the world-size events stood the microscopic one that I was doing coverage for a final newspaper column, begun in 1946, ending this same month with my 75th birthday, also the voluntary termination date of my contract.

Even a fly on the wheel of the emperor's chariot shared the exhilaration of the Roman triumph, and, I judge, the ensuing letdown. Leaving the inaugural site, I moved among people who were singing "God Bless America." With brimming eyes I thrust a handshake at a black army chaplain who returned it understandingly in the daze of fraternal patriotism brought on by Mr. Reagan's moving speech, the band and vocal music, the floating banners.

I had covered such ceremonies since 1949 without the tingles that now stirred me. A gung-ho conservative and seasoned friend of the new President, I believed the country was undergo-

153

ing a rebirth of freedom and esteem. It was a feeling that made cloudland of the turf and concrete underfoot as I hurried for my office and typewriter.

When I sat down and wrote the story for my syndicate, the realities rode in. I soon would not belong to the fourth estate of the Reagan regime; my term finished where this admired figure stepped into command. The work I had been at, virtually since separation from military service after World War II, would not be resumed. Instead, I was leaving town with my wife for a retirement vacation in Florida. Like scores of my press corps colleagues down the years, I was plunging from the peaks of excitement as a Washington and overseas correspondent into the alien abyss of no-deadline limbo. From a lower but not dissimilar level, my descent coincided with what ex-President Carter and the ex-hostages had before them—the ordeal of decompression from accustomed pressures.

Mine was not so intense nor extended as anticipated in the early moods of introspection and self-importance. The Republic would survive; the syndicate to which I felt the fond attachment of long tenure would carry on. When I telephoned New York to say goodbye to my editor, she told me:

"Don't feel sad. The stars have been good to you. In the time I know about, you lost a beloved wife and married another. You walked away from major surgery and kicked the liquor habit. You've had big moments and made many friends. This phase of your life had to pass, but there's much more to come."

Yes, I would go on writing—not knowing how to stop. Then, suddenly in the holiday sunshine, I felt the oncoming freedom such as the President had offered the citizenry. He had affirmed a liberation from the government-controlled welfare state, and a release of the people's energies into the open market.

Syndicated writing is a regulated welfare arrangement with assured publication and income as long as you hang on. At an advanced age, I was starting anew in the freelance world of ruthless competition and rejection slips, an environment where all writers begin as I had more than a half-century ago. Another Reagan admirer, Congressman Jack Kemp, one-time Buffalo Bills star quarterback, had told me when he was still a rookie:

"Professional football appeals to me as a private enterprise system. No sheltered life there. You have to meet and beat the roughest competition. No paternalism, no alibis, no results except of your own making."

So, the analogies I'd felt at the inauguration still held. Like Mr. Carter and the homecoming hostages, I would have some adjustment-making. The country and I would be on our own once again, as long ago. We'd be challenged in a freedom that was not risk-proof, but rich with the rewards of individual accomplishment.

President Reagan had called for "a new beginning," a warning of many difficulties, and that was so for me as for the nation. The release from welfarism meant the sort of freedom that Jack Kemp thought of as pro football and private enterprise. No net to catch the tumbles, no excuse for failures, but deep satisfaction for each personal achievement.

Selected Bibliography

Beard, Charles A. works of,. New York: Macmillan Publishing Co., Inc., 1930–1945.

Beard, Charles A. *An Appraisal*, ed. Howard K. Beach. Lexington, Ky.: University of Kentucky Press, 1954.

Bloomsberg, Stanley A., and Gwenn Owens. *The Life and Times of Edward Teller: Energy and Conflicts*. New York: G. P. Putnam's Sons, 1976.

Brandon, Henry. *The Retreat of American Power*. New York: Doubleday & Co., Inc., 1973.

Braun, Robert E. *Charles Beard and the Constitution*. Princeton, N.J.: Princeton University Press, 1956.

Buckley, William F., Jr., and L. Brent Bozell. *McCarthy and His Enemies*. Chicago: Henry Regnery Co., 1954.

Collins, James. *A History of Modern European Philosophy*. Milwaukee: Bruce Publishing Co., 1954.

Commager, A., ed. *Documents of American History*. Norwalk, Conn.: Appleton-Century-Crofts, 1949.

Dallek, Robert. *Franklin Roosevelt and American Foreign Policy, 1932–45*. New York: Oxford University Press, 1979.

Davis, Kenneth S. *The Hero: Charles Lindbergh and the American Dream*. New York: Doubleday & Co., Inc., 1959.

Donovan, Robert J. *Conflict and Crisis: The Presidency of Harry S. Truman, 1945–1948*. New York: W. W. Norton & Co., Inc., 1979.

Evans, Medford, and James Burnham. *The Secret War For the A-Bomb*. Chicago: Henry Regnery Co., 1953.

157

Goldwater, Barry. *With No Apologies: The Personal and Political Memoirs of a U.S. Senator*. New York: William Morrow & Co., Inc., 1979.

Karp, Walter. *The Politics of War: The Story of Two Wars Which Altered Forever the Political Life of the American Republic (1890–1920)*. New York: Harper & Row, Publishers Inc., 1979.

Lasky, Victor. *Jimmy Carter: The Man and the Myth*. New York: Richard Marek, 1979.

Lindbergh, Charles A. *The Wartime Journals of Charles A. Lindbergh*. New York: Harcourt Brace Jovanovich, 1970.

Manchester, William. *American Caesar: Douglas MacArthur 1880–1974*. Boston: Little, Brown & Co., 1978.

Maugham, Somerset. *The Summing Up*. New York: Arno Press, 1977.

Meyer, Bernard C., M.D. *Joseph Conrad: A Psychoanalytic Biography*. Princeton, N.J.: Princeton University Press, 1970.

Mosley, Leonard. *Lindbergh: A Biography*. New York: Doubleday & Co., Inc., 1976.

Phillips, Cabell. *The Truman Presidency*. New York: Macmillan Publishing Co., Inc., 1966.

Plato. *Great Dialogues of*, trans. W. H. D. Rouse. New York: New American Library, 1956.

Putnam, Carleton. *Race and Reality*. Washington, D.C.: Howard Allen, 1966.

Putnam, Carleton. *Race and Reason*. Washington, D.C.: Howard Allen, 1961.

Reeves, Thomas C. *The Life and Times of Joe McCarthy*. Briarcliff Manor, N.Y.: Stein & Day Publishers, 1982.

Regnery, Henry. *Memoirs of a Dissident Publisher*. New York: Harcourt Brace Jovanovich, 1979.

Renan, Ernest. *Life of Jesus*, trans. J. H. Holmes. New York: The Modern Library, 1927.

Rosten, Leo, ed. *Religions of America*. New York: Simon & Schuster, 1975.

Rovere, Richard. *Senator Joe McCarthy*. New York: Harper & Row, Publishers Inc., 1973.

White, F. Clifton, with William J. Gill. *Suite 3505*. New Rochelle, N.Y.: Arlington House, 1967.